Amazon Inspector User Guide

A catalogue record for this book is available from the Hong Kong Public Libraries.

Published in Hong Kong by Samurai Media Limited.

Email: info@samuraimedia.org

ISBN 9789888407774

Contents

What is Amazon Inspector?

Amazon Inspector enables you to analyze the behavior of your AWS resources and helps you to identify potential security issues. Using Amazon Inspector, you can define a collection of AWS resources that you want to include in an assessment target. You can then create an *assessment template* and launch a security *assessment run* of this target.

During the assessment run, the network, file system, and process activity within the specified target are monitored, and a wide set of activity and configuration data is collected. This data includes details of communication with AWS services, use of secure channels, details of the running processes, network traffic among the running processes, and more. The collected data is correlated, analyzed, and compared to a set of security *rules* specified in the assessment template. A completed assessment run produces a list of *findings* - potential security problems of various severity.

Important
AWS does not guarantee that following the provided recommendations will resolve every potential security issue. The findings generated by Amazon Inspector depend on your choice of rules packages included in each assessment template, the presence of non-AWS components in your system, and other factors. You are responsible for the security of applications, processes, and tools that run on AWS services. For more information, see the AWS Shared Responsibility Model for security.

Note
AWS is responsible for protecting the global infrastructure that runs all the services offered in the AWS cloud. This infrastructure comprises the hardware, software, networking, and facilities that run AWS services. AWS provides several reports from third-party auditors who have verified our compliance with a variety of computer security standards and regulations. For more information, see AWS Cloud Compliance.

For more information, see Amazon Inspector Terminology and Concepts.

Benefits of Amazon Inspector

- Amazon Inspector enables you to quickly and easily assess the security of your AWS resources for forensics, troubleshooting, or active auditing purposes at your own pace, either as you progress through the development of your infrastructures or on a regular basis in a stable production environment.
- Amazon Inspector enables you to focus on more complex security problems by offloading the overall security assessment of your infrastructure to this automated service.
- By using Amazon Inspector, you can gain deeper understanding of your AWS resources because Amazon Inspector findings are produced through the analysis of the real activity and configuration data of your AWS resources.

Features of Amazon Inspector

- **Configuration Scanning and Activity Monitoring Engine** - Amazon Inspector provides an engine that analyzes system and resource configuration and monitors activity to determine what an assessment target looks like, how it behaves, and its dependent components. The combination of this telemetry provides a complete picture of the assessment target and its potential security or compliance issues.
- **Built-in Content Library** - Amazon Inspector incorporates a built-in library of rules and reports. These include checks against best practices, common compliance standards and vulnerabilities. These checks include detailed recommended steps for resolving potential security issues.
- **Automatable via API** - Amazon Inspector is fully automatable via an API. This allows organizations to incorporate security testing into the development and design process, including selecting, executing, and reporting the results of those tests.

Amazon Inspector Pricing

Amazon Inspector is priced per agent per assessment (agent-assessment) per month. For detailed information about Amazon Inspector pricing, see Amazon Inspector Pricing.

Accessing Amazon Inspector

You can work with the Amazon Inspector service in any of the following ways.

Amazon Inspector Console

Sign in to the AWS Management Console and open the Amazon Inspector console at https://console.aws.amazon.com/inspector/.

The console is a browser-based interface to access and use the Amazon Inspector service.

AWS SDKs

AWS provides software development kits (SDKs) that consist of libraries and sample code for various programming languages and platforms (Java, Python, Ruby, .NET, iOS, Android, and more). The SDKs provide a convenient way to create programmatic access to the Amazon Inspector service. For information about the AWS SDKs, including how to download and install them, see Tools for Amazon Web Services.

Amazon Inspector HTTPS API

You can access Amazon Inspector and AWS programmatically by using the Amazon Inspector HTTPS API, which lets you issue HTTPS requests directly to the service. For more information, see the Amazon Inspector API Reference.

AWS Command Line Tools

You can use the AWS command line tools to issue commands at your system's command line to perform Amazon Inspector tasks; this can be faster and more convenient than using the console. The command line tools are also useful if you want to build scripts that perform AWS tasks. For more information, see the Amazon Inspector's AWS Command Line Interface.

Amazon Inspector Terminology and Concepts

As you get started with Amazon Inspector, you can benefit from learning about its key concepts.

Amazon Inspector Agent
A software agent that you must install on all Amazon Elastic Compute Cloud instances (EC2 instances) that are included in the assessment target, the security of which you want to evaluate with Amazon Inspector. The Amazon Inspector Agent monitors the behavior of the EC2 instance on which it is installed, including network, file system, and process activity, and collects a wide set of behavior and configuration data (telemetry), which it then passes to the Amazon Inspector service. For more information, see Amazon Inspector Agents.

Assessment run
The process of discovering potential security issues through the analysis of your assessment target's configuration and behavior against specified rules packages. During an assessment run, the agent monitors, collects, and analyzes behavioral data (telemetry) within the specified target, such as the use of secure channels, network traffic among running processes, and details of communication with AWS services. Next, Amazon Inspector analyzes the data and compares it against a set of security rules packages specified in the assessment template used during the assessment run. A completed assessment run produces a list of findings - potential security issues of various severity. For more information, see Amazon Inspector Assessment Templates and Assessment Runs.

Assessment target
In the context of Amazon Inspector, a collection of AWS resources that work together as a unit to help you accomplish your business goals. Amazon Inspector evaluates the security state of the resources that constitute the assessment target.
At this time, your Amazon Inspector assessment targets can consist only of EC2 instances. For more information, see Amazon Inspector Service Limits To create an Amazon Inspector assessment target, you must first tag your EC2 instances with key-value pairs of your choice, and then create a view of these tagged EC2 instances that have common keys or common values. For more information, see Amazon Inspector Assessment Targets.

Assessment template
A configuration that is used during your assessment run, including rules packages against which you want Amazon Inspector to evaluate your assessment target, the duration of the assessment run, Amazon Simple Notification Service (SNS) topics to which you want Amazon Inspector to send notifications about assessment run states and findings, and Amazon Inspector-specific attributes (key-value pairs) that you can assign to findings generated by the assessment run that uses this assessment template.

Finding
A potential security issue discovered during the Amazon Inspector assessment run of the specified target. Findings are displayed in the Amazon Inspector console or retrieved through the API, and contain both a detailed description of the security issue and a recommendation on how to fix it. For more information, see Amazon Inspector Findings.

Rule
In the context of Amazon Inspector, a security check that the agent performs during an assessment run. When a rule detects a potential security issue, Amazon Inspector generates a finding that describes the issue.

Rules package
In the context of Amazon Inspector, a collection of rules. A rules package corresponds to a security goal that you might have. You can specify your security goal by selecting the appropriate rules package when you create an Amazon Inspector assessment template. For more information, see Amazon Inspector Rules Packages and Rules.

Telemetry
Data (behavioral, configuration, etc.) such as records of network connections and process creations, collected by the Amazon Inspector Agent on your EC2 instances during an assessment run and passed to the Amazon Inspector service for analysis.

Amazon Inspector Service Limits

Amazon Inspector evaluates the security state of the resources that constitute the assessment target.

Important
At this time, your Amazon Inspector assessment targets can consist only of EC2 instances.

The following are Amazon Inspector limits per AWS account:

Resource	Default Limit	Comments
Agents per assessment	500	The maximum number of agents that can be included in the assessment target of an assessment run. You can request a limit increase of agents per assessment by contacting AWS customer support.
Assessment runs	50000	The maximum number of assessment runs that you can create per AWS account. You can have multiple assessment runs happening at the same time as long as the assessment targets used for these runs do not contain overlapping EC2 instances. You can request a limit increase of assessment runs by contacting AWS customer support.
Assessment templates	500	The maximum number of assessment templates that you can have at any given time in an AWS account. You can request a limit increase of assessment templates by contacting AWS customer support.
Assessment targets	50	The maximum number of assessment targets that you can have at any given time in an AWS account. You can request a limit increase of assessment targets by contacting AWS customer support.

Amazon Inspector Supported Operating Systems and Regions

Amazon Inspector evaluates the security state of the resources that constitute the assessment target.

Important
At this time, your Amazon Inspector assessment targets can consist only of EC2 instances.

Note
For information on how Amazon Inspector rules packages are available across supported operating systems that you can run on the EC2 instances included in your assessment targets, see Rules Packages Availability Across Supported Operating Systems.

Topics

- Supported Linux-based Operating Systems
- Supported Windows-based Operating Systems
- Supported Regions

Supported Linux-based Operating Systems

In this release of Amazon Inspector, your assessment targets can consist only of EC2 instances that run the 64-bit version of the following Linux-based operating systems:

- Amazon Linux 2 (2017.12)
- Amazon Linux (2018.03, 2017.09, 2017.03, 2016.09, 2016.03, 2015.09, 2015.03, 2014.09, 2014.03, 2013.09, 2013.03, 2012.09, 2012.03)
- Ubuntu (18.04 LTS, 16.04 LTS, 14.04 LTS)
- Debian (9.0 - 9.4)
- Red Hat Enterprise Linux (7.2 - 7.5, 6.2 - 6.9)
- CentOS (7.2 - 7.5, 6.2 - 6.9)

Important
The following list contains all kernel versions that are compatible with the Amazon Inspector Agent running on Linux, Ubuntu, Red Hat Enterprise Linux, and CentOS: https://s3.amazonaws.com/aws-agent.us-east-1/linux/support/supported_versions.json.
You can run a successful Amazon Inspector assessment of an EC2 instance with a Linux-based OS using either the CVE, CIS, or Security Best Practices rules packages even if your instance does not have a kernel version that is included in this list.
To run a successful Amazon Inspector assessment of an EC2 instance with a Linux-based OS using the Runtime Behavior Analysis rules package, your instance must have a kernel version that is included in this list. If your instance has a kernel version that is not compatible with the Amazon Inspector Agent, the Runtime Behavior Analysis rules package assessing that EC2 instance results in only one informational finding informing you that the kernel version of your EC2 instance is not supported.

Supported Windows-based Operating Systems

In this release of Amazon Inspector, your assessment targets can consist only of EC2 instances that run the 64-bit version of the following Windows-based operating systems:

- Windows Server 2008 R2
- Windows Server 2012
- Windows Server 2012 R2
- Windows Server 2016 Base

Supported Regions

- Asia Pacific (Mumbai)
- Asia Pacific (Seoul)
- Asia Pacific (Sydney)
- Asia Pacific (Tokyo)
- EU (Frankfurt)
- EU (Ireland)
- US East (Northern Virginia)
- US East (Ohio)
- US West (Northern California)
- US West (Oregon)
- AWS GovCloud (US)

Setting up Amazon Inspector

When you sign up for Amazon Web Services (AWS), your AWS account is automatically signed up for all services in AWS, including Amazon Inspector. If you don't have an AWS account, use the following procedure to create one.

To sign up for AWS

1. Open https://aws.amazon.com/, and then choose **Create an AWS Account. Note**
   This might be unavailable in your browser if you previously signed into the AWS Management Console. In that case, choose **Sign in to a different account**, and then choose **Create a new AWS account**.

2. Follow the online instructions.

   Part of the sign-up procedure involves receiving a phone call and entering a PIN using the phone keypad.

When you launch the Amazon Inspector console for the first time, choose **Get Started** and complete the following prerequisite tasks. You must complete these tasks before you can create, start, and complete an Amazon Inspector assessment run:

- Tag all EC2 instances that you want to include in your assessment target
- Install the Amazon Inspector Agent on all EC2 instances that you want to include in your assessment target

Important
Amazon Inspector is granted access to your resources through an IAM service-linked role called `AWSServiceRoleForAmazonInspector`. For more information, see Auto-create a service-linked role to grant Amazon Inspector access your AWS account.

Create Assessment Targets with EC2 instance Tags

Amazon Inspector evaluates whether your assessment targets (collections of AWS resources) have potential security issues.

Important
In this release of Amazon Inspector, your assessment targets can consist only of EC2 instances that run on a number of supported operating systems. For more information about supported Linux-based and Windows-based operating systems, and supported AWS regions, see Amazon Inspector Supported Operating Systems and Regions.
For more information about launching EC2 instances, see Amazon Elastic Compute Cloud Documentation.

Amazon Inspector uses the tags applied to your EC2 instances to target those resources as part of your defined assessment template. When configuring your assessment targets, you can utilize the tags you already have defined on your EC2 instances, or create entirely new tags specifically for your assessments. For more information about tagging, see Working with Tag Editor and Tagging Your Amazon EC2 Resources.

For more information about tagging EC2 instances to be included in Amazon Inspector assessment targets, see Amazon Inspector Assessment Targets.

Install the Amazon Inspector Agent

You must install the Amazon Inspector Agent on each EC2 instance in your assessment target. The agent monitors the behavior of the EC2 instances on which it is installed, including network, file system, and process activity, and collects a wide set of behavior and configuration data (telemetry), which it then passes to the Amazon Inspector service. For more information about Amazon Inspector Agent privileges, security, updates, telemetry data, and access control, see Amazon Inspector Agents.

For more information about how to install the Amazon Inspector Agent, see Installing Amazon Inspector Agents. For more information about how to uninstall the agent or verify whether the installed agent is running, see Working with Amazon Inspector Agents on Linux-based Operating Systems and Working with Amazon Inspector Agents on Windows-based Operating Systems.

Important

To skip the manual Amazon Inspector Agent installation on the Amazon Linux EC2 instances that you want to include in your assessment targets, you can use the ** Amazon Linux AMI with Amazon Inspector Agent**. This AMI has the Amazon Inspector Agent pre-installed and requires no additional steps to install or setup the agent. To start using Amazon Inspector with these EC2 instances, simply tag them to match the desired assessment target. The configuration of ** Amazon Linux AMI with Amazon Inspector Agent** enhances security by focusing on two main security goals: limiting access and reducing software vulnerabilities.

This is the only currently available EC2 instance AMI with the pre-installed Amazon Inspector Agent. For the EC2 instances running Ubuntu Server or Windows Server, you must complete the manual Amazon Inspector Agent installation steps.

The ** Amazon Linux AMI with Amazon Inspector Agent** is available in the EC2 console and also the AWS Marketplace.

Auto-create a service-linked role to grant Amazon Inspector access your AWS account

Amazon Inspector needs to enumerate your EC2 instances and tags to identify the EC2 instances specified in the assessment targets. Amazon Inspector gets access to these resources in your AWS account through a service-linked role called `AWSServiceRoleForAmazonInspector`. A service-linked role is a unique type of IAM role that is linked directly to an AWS service (in this case, Amazon Inspector). Service-linked roles are predefined by the service and include all the permissions that the service requires to call other AWS services on your behalf. The linked service (in this case, Amazon Inspector) also defines how you create, modify, and delete a service-linked role. For more information about service-linked roles, see Using Service-Linked Roles for Amazon Inspector and Using Service-Linked Roles.

For the `AWSServiceRoleForAmazonInspector` service-linked role to be successfully created, the IAM identity (user, role, group) with which you use Amazon Inspector, must have the required permissions. To grant the required permissions, attach the **AmazonInspectorFullAccess** managed policy to this IAM user, group, or role. For more information, see AWS Managed (Predefined) Policies for Amazon Inspector.

The `AWSServiceRoleForAmazonInspector` service-linked role is created automatically. The following sections describe the details of auto-generating and using the `AWSServiceRoleForAmazonInspector` service-linked role when you get started with Amazon Inspector for the first time or when you already have Amazon Inspector running in your AWS account.

If you are getting started with Amazon Inspector for the first time

- The `AWSServiceRoleForAmazonInspector` service-linked role is created automatically when you go through the **Get Started with Amazon Inspector** wizard in the console or when you run the CreateAssessmentTarget API operation.
- The `AWSServiceRoleForAmazonInspector` service-linked role is created for your AWS account only in the region to which you are currently signed in. It grants Amazon Inspector access to the resources in your AWS account only in this region. If you then use the same AWS account to go through the **Get Started with Amazon Inspector** console wizard or run the CreateAssessmentTarget API operation in other regions, the same service-linked role that is already created in your AWS account is applied in these other regions and grants Amazon Inspector access to the resources in your AWS account in these other regions.

If you already have Amazon Inspector running in your AWS account

- If you already have Amazon Inspector running in your AWS account, the IAM role that grants Amazon Inspector access to your resources already exists in your AWS account. In this case, the `AWSServiceRoleForAmazonInspector` service-linked role is auto-created when you create a new assessment target or a new assessment template (either through the Amazon Inspector console or the API operations). This newly created service-linked role replaces the previously created IAM role that up until now granted Amazon Inspector access to your resources.

  You can also create the `AWSServiceRoleForAmazonInspector` service-linked role manually by choosing the **Manage Amazon Inspector service-linked role** link in the **Accounts Setting** section in the Inspector's **Dashboard** page. This newly created service-linked role replaces the previously created IAM role that up until now granted Amazon Inspector access to your resources. **Note**
  This previously created IAM role is not deleted. It remains intact, but it is no longer used to grant Amazon Inspector access to your resources. You can use the IAM console to further manage or delete this IAM role.

- The `AWSServiceRoleForAmazonInspector` service-linked role is created for your AWS account only in the region to which you are currently signed in. It grants Amazon Inspector access to the resources in your AWS account only in this region. If you then use the same AWS account to create a new assessment target or a new assessment template for your Amazon Inspector service running in other regions, the same service-linked role that is already created in your AWS account is applied and grants Amazon Inspector access to the resources in your AWS account in these other regions.

To delete the `AWSServiceRoleForAmazonInspector` service-linked role, you must first delete your assessment targets for this AWS account in all the regions where you have Amazon Inspector running. You can delete the `AWSServiceRoleForAmazonInspector` service-linked role through the IAM console. For more information, see Using Service-Linked Roles.

Using Service-Linked Roles for Amazon Inspector

Amazon Inspector uses AWS Identity and Access Management (IAM) service-linked roles. A service-linked role is a unique type of IAM role that is linked directly to Amazon Inspector. Service-linked roles are predefined by Amazon Inspector and include all the permissions that the service requires to call other AWS services on your behalf.

A service-linked role makes setting up Amazon Inspector easier because you don't have to manually add the necessary permissions. Amazon Inspector defines the permissions of its service-linked roles, and unless defined otherwise, only Amazon Inspector can assume its roles. The defined permissions include the trust policy and the permissions policy, and that permissions policy cannot be attached to any other IAM entity.

You can delete a service-linked role only after first deleting your assessment targets for a AWS account in all the regions where you have Amazon Inspector running.

For information about other services that support service-linked roles, see AWS Services That Work with IAM and look for the services that have **Yes **in the **Service-Linked Role** column. Choose a **Yes** with a link to view the service-linked role documentation for that service.

For more information, see Auto-create a service-linked role to grant Amazon Inspector access your AWS account.

Service-Linked Role Permissions for Amazon Inspector

Amazon Inspector uses the service-linked role named **AWSServiceRoleForAmazonInspector**.

The AWSServiceRoleForAmazonInspector service-linked role trusts the following services to assume the role:

- `Amazon Inspector`

The role permissions policy allows Amazon Inspector to complete the following actions on the specified resources:

- Action: `iam:CreateServiceLinkedRole` on `arn:aws:iam::*:role/aws-service-role/inspector.amazonaws.com/AWSServiceRoleForAmazonInspector`

For the `AWSServiceRoleForAmazonInspector` service-linked role to be successfully created, the IAM identity (user, role, group) with which you use Amazon Inspector, must have the required permissions. To grant the required permissions, attach the **AmazonInspectorFullAccess** managed policy to this IAM user, group, or role. For more information, see AWS Managed (Predefined) Policies for Amazon Inspector.

For more information, see Service-Linked Role Permissions in the *IAM User Guide.*

Creating a Service-Linked Role for Amazon Inspector

You don't need to manually create the `AWSServiceRoleForAmazonInspector` service-linked role.

The `AWSServiceRoleForAmazonInspector` service-linked role is created automatically. The following sections describe the details of auto-generating and using the `AWSServiceRoleForAmazonInspector` service-linked role when you get started with Amazon Inspector for the first time or when you already have Amazon Inspector running in your AWS account.

If you are getting started with Amazon Inspector for the first time

- The `AWSServiceRoleForAmazonInspector` service-linked role is created automatically when you go through the **Get Started with Amazon Inspector** wizard in the console or when you run the CreateAssessmentTarget API operation.

17

- The `AWSServiceRoleForAmazonInspector` service-linked role is created for your AWS account only in the region to which you are currently signed in. It grants Amazon Inspector access to the resources in your AWS account only in this region. If you then use the same AWS account to go through the **Get Started with Amazon Inspector** console wizard or run the CreateAssessmentTarget API operation in other regions, the same service-linked role that is already created in your AWS account is applied in these other regions and grants Amazon Inspector access to the resources in your AWS account in these other regions.

If you already have Amazon Inspector running in your AWS account

- If you already have Amazon Inspector running in your AWS account, the IAM role that grants Amazon Inspector access to your resources already exists in your AWS account. In this case, the `AWSServiceRoleForAmazonInspector` service-linked role is auto-created when you create a new assessment target or a new assessment template (either through the Amazon Inspector console or the API operations). This newly created service-linked role replaces the previously created IAM role that up until now granted Amazon Inspector access to your resources.

  You can also create the `AWSServiceRoleForAmazonInspector` service-linked role manually by choosing the **Manage Amazon Inspector service-linked role** link in the **Accounts Setting** section in the Inspector's **Dashboard** page. This newly created service-linked role replaces the previously created IAM role that up until now granted Amazon Inspector access to your resources. **Note**
  This previously created IAM role is not deleted. It remains intact, but it is no longer used to grant Amazon Inspector access to your resources. You can use the IAM console to further manage or delete this IAM role.

- The `AWSServiceRoleForAmazonInspector` service-linked role is created for your AWS account only in the region to which you are currently signed in. It grants Amazon Inspector access to the resources in your AWS account only in this region. If you then use the same AWS account to create a new assessment target or a new assessment template for your Amazon Inspector service running in other regions, the same service-linked role that is already created in your AWS account is applied and grants Amazon Inspector access to the resources in your AWS account in these other regions.

You can also use the IAM console to create a service-linked role with the **Inspector** use case. In the IAM CLI or the IAM API, create a service-linked role with the `Amazon Inspector` service name. For more information, see Creating a Service-Linked Role in the *IAM User Guide*.

If you delete this service-linked role, and then need to create it again, you can use the same process to recreate the role in your account. When you Get started with Amazon Inspector again, the service-linked role is automatically created for you again.

Editing a Service-Linked Role for Amazon Inspector

Amazon Inspector does not allow you to edit the AWSServiceRoleForAmazonInspector service-linked role. After you create a service-linked role, you cannot change the name of the role because various entities might reference the role. However, you can edit the description of the role using IAM. For more information, see Editing a Service-Linked Role in the *IAM User Guide*.

Deleting a Service-Linked Role for Amazon Inspector

If you no longer need to use a feature or service that requires a service-linked role, we recommend that you delete that role. That way you don't have an unused entity that is not actively monitored or maintained. However, you must clean up the resources for your service-linked role before you can manually delete it.

Note
If the Amazon Inspector service is using the role when you try to delete the resources, then the deletion might fail. If that happens, wait for a few minutes and try the operation again.

To delete Amazon Inspector resources used by the AWSServiceRoleForAmazonInspector

- Delete your assessment targets for this AWS account in all the regions where you have Amazon Inspector running. For more information, see Amazon Inspector Assessment Targets.

To manually delete the service-linked role using IAM

Use the IAM console, the IAM CLI, or the IAM API to delete the AWSServiceRoleForAmazonInspector service-linked role. For more information, see Deleting a Service-Linked Role in the *IAM User Guide*.

Amazon Inspector Quickstart Walkthrough - Red Hat Enterprise Linux

Before you follow the instructions in this walkthrough, we recommend that you get familiar with the Amazon Inspector Terminology and Concepts.

This walkthrough is designed for a first-time user and includes all the tasks, including prerequisite tasks, for creating an assessment target, assessment template, and assessment run.

This walkthrough is designed to demonstrate how to use Amazon Inspector to analyze the behavior of the EC2 instances that run the Red Hat Enterprise Linux 7.4 operating system.

- Set Up Amazon Inspector. This is the first-run experience, including completing all the pre-requisite tasks via the Amazon Inspector console.
- Prepare Your Assessment Target for the Assessment Run
- Create an Assessment Target
- Create and Run an Assessment Template
- Locate and Analyze Generated Findings
- Apply the Recommended Fix to Your Assessment Target

Set Up Amazon Inspector

1. Sign in to the AWS Management Console and open the Amazon Inspector console at https://console.aws.amazon.com/inspector/.

2. Choose **Get started** to launch the **Get started** wizard, and on the **Step 1: Prerequisites** page, do the following:

   1. Tag the EC2 instances that you want to include in your Amazon Inspector assessment target.

      For this walkthrough, create one EC2 instance running Red Hat Enterprise Linux 7.4 and tag it using the **Name** key and a value of **InspectorEC2InstanceLinux**. **Note**
      For more information about tagging EC2 instances, see Resources and Tags.

   2. Install the Amazon Inspector Agent on your tagged EC2 instance. **Note**
      You can install the Amazon Inspector Agent on multiple instances (both Linux-based and Windows-based with the same command) at once using the Systems Manager Run Command. To install the agent on all the instances in the assessment target, you can specify the same tags used for creating the assessment target. Or you can install the Amazon Inspector Agent on your EC2 instance manually. For more information, see Installing Amazon Inspector Agents.

   3. Choose **Next**.

Note
At this point, a service-linked role called `AWSServiceRoleForAmazonInspector` is created to grant Amazon Inspector access to your resources. For more information, see Auto-create a service-linked role to grant Amazon Inspector access your AWS account.

Prepare Your Assessment Target for the Assessment Run

For this walkthrough, you modify your assessment target to expose it to the potential security issue CVE-2018-5732. For more information, see https://cve.mitre.org/cgi-bin/cvename.cgi?name=CVE-2018-5732. Also, for more information, see Common Vulnerabilities and Exposures.

Connect to your instance **InspectorEC2InstanceLinux** that you created in the preceding section, and run the following command:

```
sudo yum install dhclient-4.2.5-58.el7.x86_64
```

Create an Assessment Target

On the **Amazon Inspector - Assessment Targets ** page, choose **Create** and then do the following:

1. For **Name**, type the name for your assessment target.

   For this walkthrough, type **MyTargetLinux**.

2. Use the **Tags Key** and **Value** fields to type the tag key name and key-value pairs in order to select the EC2 instances that you want to include in this assessment target.

   For this walkthrough, to use the EC2 instance that you created in the preceding step, type **Name** in the **Key** field and **InspectorEC2InstanceLinux** in the **Value** field, and then choose **Save**.

Create and Run an Assessment Template

On the **Amazon Inspector - Assessment Templates ** page, choose **Create** and then do the following:

1. For **Name**, type the name for your assessment template. For this walkthrough, type **MyFirstTemplateLinux**.

2. For **Target name**, choose the assessment target you created above - **MyTargetLinux**.

3. For **Rules packages**, use the pull-down menu to select the rules packages that you want to use in this assessment template.

   For this walkthrough, choose **Common Vulnerabilities and Exposures-1.1**.

4. For **Duration**, specify the duration for your assessment template.

   For this walkthrough, select **15 minutes**.

5. Choose **Create and run**.

Locate and Analyze Generated Findings

A completed assessment run produces a set of findings, or potential security issues that Amazon Inspector discovered in your assessment target. You can review the findings and follow the recommended steps to resolve the potential security issues.

In this walkthrough, if you complete the preceding steps, your assessment run produces a finding against the common vulnerability CVE-2018-5732.

1. Navigate to the **Amazon Inspector - Assessment Runs** page in the Amazon Inspector console and verify that the status of run for the assessment template called **MyFirstTemplateLinux** that you created in the preceding step is set to **Collecting data**. This indicates that the assessment run is currently in progress, and the telemetry data for your target is being collected and analyzed against the selected rules packages.

2. You cannot view the findings generated by the assessment run while it is still in progress. Let the assessment run complete its entire duration. However, for this walkthrough, you can stop the run after several minutes.

   Note that the status of **MyFirstTemplateLinux** changes first to **Stopping**, then in a few minutes to **Analyzing**, and then finally to **Analysis complete**. To see this change in status, you can choose the **Refresh** icon.

21

3. In the Amazon Inspector console, navigate to the **Amazon Inspector - Findings** page.

You can see a new finding of High severity that reads "Instance InspectorEC2InstanceLinux is vulnerable to CVE-2018-5732". **Note**
If you do not see the new finding, choose the **Refresh** icon.

To expand the view and see the details of this finding, choose the arrow to the left of the finding. The details of the finding include the following:

- The ARN of the finding
- The name of the assessment run that produced this finding
- The name of the assessment target that produced this finding
- The name of the assessment template that produced this finding
- The assessment run start time
- The assessment run end time
- The assessment run status
- The name of the rules package that includes the rule that triggered this finding
- The Amazon Inspector Agent ID
- The name of the finding
- The severity of the finding
- The description of the finding
- The recommended remediation steps that you can complete to fix the potential security issue described by the finding

Apply the Recommended Fix to Your Assessment Target

For this walkthrough, you modified your assessment target to expose it to a potential security issue CVE-2018-5732. In this procedure, you can apply the recommended fix for this issue.

1. Connect to your instance **InspectorEC2InstanceLinux** that you created in the preceding section, and run the following command:

```
sudo yum update dhclient
```

2. On the **Amazon Inspector - Assessment Templates** page, select **MyFirstTemplateLinux**, and then choose **Run** to start a new assessment run using this template.

3. Follow the steps in Locate and Analyze Generated Findings to see the findings resulting from this subsequent run of the **MyFirstTemplateLinux** template.

Because you resolved the found CVE-2018-5732 security issue, you will no longer see a finding highlighting it.

Amazon Inspector Quickstart Walkthrough - Ubuntu Server

Before you follow the instructions in this walkthrough, we recommend that you get familiar with the Amazon Inspector Terminology and Concepts.

This walkthrough is designed for a first-time user and includes all the tasks, including prerequisite tasks, for creating an assessment target, assessment template, and assessment run.

This walkthrough is designed to demonstrate how to use Amazon Inspector to analyze the behavior of the EC2 instances that run the Ubuntu Server 16.04 LTS operating system.

- Set Up Amazon Inspector. This is the first-run experience, including completing all the pre-requisite tasks via the Amazon Inspector console.
- Prepare Your Assessment Target for the Assessment Run
- Create an Assessment Target
- Create and Run an Assessment Template
- Locate and Analyze Generated Findings
- Apply the Recommended Fix to Your Assessment Target

Set Up Amazon Inspector

1. Sign in to the AWS Management Console and open the Amazon Inspector console at https://console.aws.amazon.com/inspector/.

2. Choose **Get started** to launch the **Get started** wizard, and on the **Step 1: Prerequisites** page, do the following:

   1. Tag the EC2 instances that you want to include in your Amazon Inspector assessment target.

      For this walkthrough, create one EC2 instance running Ubuntu Server 16.04 LTS and tag it using the **Name** key and a value of **InspectorEC2InstanceUbuntu**. **Note**
      For more information about tagging EC2 instances, see Resources and Tags.

   2. Install the Amazon Inspector Agent on your tagged EC2 instance. **Note**
      You can install the Amazon Inspector Agent on multiple instances (both Linux-based and Windows-based with the same command) at once using the Systems Manager Run Command. To install the agent on all the instances in the assessment target, you can specify the same tags used for creating the assessment target. Or you can install the Amazon Inspector Agent on your EC2 instance manually. For more information, see Installing Amazon Inspector Agents.

   3. Choose **Next**.

Note
At this point, a service-linked role called `AWSServiceRoleForAmazonInspector` is created to grant Amazon Inspector access to your resources. For more information, see Auto-create a service-linked role to grant Amazon Inspector access your AWS account.

Prepare Your Assessment Target for the Assessment Run

For this walkthrough, you modify your assessment target to expose it to the potential security issue CVE-2017-6507. For more information, see https://cve.mitre.org/cgi-bin/cvename.cgi?name=CVE-2017-6507. Also, for more information, see Common Vulnerabilities and Exposures.

Connect to your instance **InspectorEC2InstanceUbuntu** that you created in the preceding section, and run the following command:

```
sudo apt-get install apparmor=2.10.95-0ubuntu2.5
```

Create an Assessment Target

On the **Amazon Inspector - Assessment Targets ** page, choose **Create** and then do the following:

1. For **Name**, type the name for your assessment target.

   For this walkthrough, type **MyTargetUbuntu**.

2. Use the **Tags Key** and **Value** fields to type the tag key name and key-value pairs in order to select the EC2 instances that you want to include in this assessment target.

   For this walkthrough, to use the EC2 instance that you created in the preceding step, type **Name** in the **Key** field and **InspectorEC2InstanceUbuntu** in the **Value** field, and then choose **Save**.

Create and Run an Assessment Template

On the **Amazon Inspector - Assessment Templates ** page, choose **Create** and then do the following:

1. For **Name**, type the name for your assessment template. For this walkthrough, type **MyFirstTemplateUbuntu**.

2. For **Target name**, choose the assessment target you created above - **MyTargetUbuntu**.

3. For **Rules packages**, use the pull-down menu to select the rules packages that you want to use in this assessment template.

   For this walkthrough, choose **Common Vulnerabilities and Exposures-1.1**.

4. For **Duration**, specify the duration for your assessment template.

   For this walkthrough, select **15 minutes**.

5. Choose **Create and run**.

Locate and Analyze Generated Findings

A completed assessment run produces a set of findings, or potential security issues that Amazon Inspector discovered in your assessment target. You can review the findings and follow the recommended steps to resolve the potential security issues.

In this walkthrough, if you complete the preceding steps, your assessment run produces a finding against the common vulnerability CVE-2017-6507.

1. Navigate to the **Amazon Inspector - Assessment Runs** page in the Amazon Inspector console and verify that the status of run for the assessment template called **MyFirstTemplateUbuntu** that you created in the preceding step is set to **Collecting data**. This indicates that the assessment run is currently in progress, and the telemetry data for your target is being collected and analyzed against the selected rules packages.

2. You cannot view the findings generated by the assessment run while it is still in progress. Let the assessment run complete its entire duration.

   Note that the status of **MyFirstTemplateUbuntu** changes first to **Stopping**, then in a few minutes to **Analyzing**, and then finally to **Analysis complete**. To see this change in status, you can choose the **Refresh** icon.

3. In the Amazon Inspector console, navigate to the **Amazon Inspector - Findings** page.

   You can see a new finding of High severity that reads "Instance InspectorEC2InstanceLinux is vulnerable to CVE-2017-6507". **Note**
   If you do not see the new finding, choose the **Refresh** icon.

To expand the view and see the details of this finding, choose the arrow to the left of the finding. The details of the finding include the following:

- The ARN of the finding
- The name of the assessment run that produced this finding
- The name of the assessment target that produced this finding
- The name of the assessment template that produced this finding
- The assessment run start time
- The assessment run end time
- The assessment run status
- The name of the rules package that includes the rule that triggered this finding
- The Amazon Inspector Agent ID
- The name of the finding
- The severity of the finding
- The description of the finding
- The recommended remediation steps that you can complete to fix the potential security issue described by the finding

Apply the Recommended Fix to Your Assessment Target

For this walkthrough, you modified your assessment target to expose it to a potential security issue CVE-2017-6507. In this procedure, you can apply the recommended fix for this issue.

1. Connect to your instance **InspectorEC2InstanceLinux** that you created in the preceding section, and run the following command:

   ```
   sudo apt-get install apparmor=2.10.95-0ubuntu2.6
   ```

2. On the **Amazon Inspector - Assessment Templates** page, select **MyFirstTemplateUbuntu**, and then choose **Run** to start a new assessment run using this template.

3. Follow the steps in Locate and Analyze Generated Findings to see the findings resulting from this subsequent run of the **MyFirstTemplateUbuntu** template.

   Because you resolved the found CVE-2017-6507 security issue, you will no longer see a finding highlighting it.

Amazon Inspector Agents

To assess the security of the EC2 instances that make up your Amazon Inspector assessment targets, you must install the Amazon Inspector Agent on each instance. The agent monitors the behavior (including network, file system, and process activity) of the EC2 instance on which it is installed, collects behavior and configuration data (telemetry), and then passes the data to the Amazon Inspector service.

For more information about how to install, uninstall, and reinstall the Amazon Inspector Agent, how to verify whether the installed agent is running, and how to configure proxy support for the Amazon Inspector Agents, see Working with Amazon Inspector Agents on Linux-based Operating Systems and Working with Amazon Inspector Agents on Windows-based Operating Systems.

Topics
- Amazon Inspector Agent Privileges
- Network and Amazon Inspector Agent Security
- Amazon Inspector Agent Updates
- Telemetry Data Lifecycle
- Access Control from Amazon Inspector into AWS Accounts
- Amazon Inspector Agent Limits
- Amazon Inspector Agent Public Licensing
- Installing Amazon Inspector Agents
- Working with Amazon Inspector Agents on Linux-based Operating Systems
- Working with Amazon Inspector Agents on Windows-based Operating Systems
- (Optional) Verify the Signature of the Amazon Inspector Agent Installation Script on Linux-based Operating Systems
- (Optional) Verify the Signature of the Amazon Inspector Agent Installation Script on Windows-based Operating Systems

Amazon Inspector Agent Privileges

Administrative or root permissions are required to install the Amazon Inspector Agent. On supported Linux-based operating systems, the Amazon Inspector Agent consists of a user mode executable that runs with root access and a kernel module that is required for the agent to function. On supported Windows-based operating systems, the agent consists of an updater service and an agent service, each running in user mode with LocalSystem privileges, and a kernel mode driver that is required for the agent to function.

Important
The following list contains all kernel versions that are compatible with the Amazon Inspector Agent running on Linux, Ubuntu, Red Hat Enterprise Linux, and CentOS: https://s3.amazonaws.com/aws-agent.us-east-1/linux/support/supported_versions.json.
You can run a successful Amazon Inspector assessment of an EC2 instance with a Linux-based OS using either the CVE, CIS, or Security Best Practices rules packages even if your instance does not have a kernel version that is included in this list.
To run a successful Amazon Inspector assessment of an EC2 instance with a Linux-based OS using the Runtime Behavior Analysis rules package, your instance must have a kernel version that is included in this list. If your instance has a kernel version that is not compatible with the Amazon Inspector Agent, the Runtime Behavior Analysis rules package assessing that EC2 instance results in only one informational finding informing you that the kernel version of your EC2 instance is not supported.

Network and Amazon Inspector Agent Security

All communication between the Amazon Inspector Agent and Amazon Inspector is initiated by the Amazon Inspector Agent. As such, the agent must have an outbound network path to the public endpoint for sending telemetry data from the Amazon Inspector Agent (arsenal..amazonaws.com) and Amazon S3 services (s3.dual-stack.aws-region.amazonaws.com). (Make sure to replace with the actual AWS region where you have Amazon Inspector running.) For more information, see AWS IP Address Ranges. Additionally, as all connections from the agent are established outbound, it is not necessary to open ports in your security groups to allow inbound communications to the agent from Amazon Inspector.

The Amazon Inspector Agent periodically communicates with Amazon Inspector over a TLS-protected channel which is authenticated using either the AWS identity associated with the role of the EC2 instance, if present, or with the instance metadata document if no role is assigned to the instance. Once authenticated, the agent sends heartbeat messages to the service and receives instructions from the service as responses to the heartbeat messages. If an assessment has been scheduled, the agent receives the instructions for that assessment. These instructions are structured JSON files and tell the agent to enable or disable specific pre-configured sensors in the agent. Each instruction action is pre-defined within the agent and arbitrary instructions cannot be executed.

During an assessment, the agent gathers telemetry data from the system to send back to Amazon Inspector over a TLS-protected channel. The agent does not make changes to the system that it collects data from. Once collected, the agent sends the telemetry data back to Amazon Inspector for processing. Beyond the telemetry data that it generates, the agent is not capable of collecting or transmitting any other data about the system or assessment targets that it is assessing. At present, there is no method exposed for intercepting and examining telemetry data at the agent.

Amazon Inspector Agent Updates

As updates for the Amazon Inspector Agent become available, they are automatically downloaded from Amazon S3 and applied. This will also update any required dependencies. The auto-update feature eliminates the need for you to track and manually maintain the versioning of the agents that you have installed on your EC2 instances. All updates are subject to audited Amazon change control processes to ensure compliance with applicable security standards. To further ensure the security of the agent, all communication between the agent and the auto-update release site (S3) are performed over a TLS connection, and the server is authenticated. All binaries involved in the auto-update process are digitally signed and the signatures are verified by the updater prior to installation. The auto-update process is executed only during non-assessment periods, and the update process has the ability to rollback and retry the update if any errors are detected. Finally, the agent update process serves to only upgrade the agent capabilities, and none of your specific information is ever sent from the agent to Amazon Inspector as part of the update workflow. The only information communicated as part of the update process is the basic installation success/fail telemetry and, if applicable, any update failure diagnostic information.

Telemetry Data Lifecycle

The telemetry data generated by the Amazon Inspector Agent during assessment runs is formatted in JSON files and delivered in near-real-time over TLS to Amazon Inspector, where it is encrypted with a per-assessment-run, ephemeral KMS-derived key and securely stored in an S3 bucket dedicated for Amazon Inspector. The rules engine of Amazon Inspector's accesses the encrypted telemetry data in the S3 bucket, decrypts it in memory, and processes the data against the configured assessment rules to generate findings. The telemetry data stored in S3 is retained only to allow for assistance with support requests and is not used or aggregated by Amazon for any other purpose. After 30 days, telemetry data is permanently deleted per a standard Amazon Inspector-dedicated S3 bucket lifecycle policy. At present, Amazon Inspector does not provide an API or an S3 bucket access mechanism to collected telemetry.

Access Control from Amazon Inspector into AWS Accounts

As a security service, Amazon Inspector accesses your AWS accounts and resources only when it needs to find EC2 instances to assess by querying for tags. It does this through standard IAM access by the role created during the initial setup of the Amazon Inspector service. During an assessment, all communications with your environment are initiated by the Amazon Inspector Agent that is installed locally on EC2 instances. The Amazon Inspector service objects that are created, such as assessment targets, assessment templates, and findings generated by the service, are stored in a database managed by and accessible only to Amazon Inspector.

Amazon Inspector Agent Limits

For information about Amazon Inspector Agent limits, see Amazon Inspector Service Limits.

Amazon Inspector Agent Public Licensing

The Amazon Inspector Agent used in conjunction with Amazon Inspector, utilizes a Kernel module (amznmon64) as a component of the overall agent. This Kernel module uses a general public license (GPLv2). The module source code and licensing information are publicly available and can be accessed at:

- Source code: https://s3.amazonaws.com/aws-agent.us-east-1/linux/support/AwsAgentKernelModule.tar.gz
- Signature file: https://s3.amazonaws.com/aws-agent.us-east-1/linux/support/AwsAgentKernelModule.tar.gz.sig

Installing Amazon Inspector Agents

The Amazon Inspector Agent can be installed using the Systems Manager Run Command on multiple instances (including both Linux-based and Windows-based instances), or individually by signing in to each EC2 instance. The procedures below provide instructions for both methods.

Topics

- Amazon Linux AMI with Amazon Inspector Agent
- To install the Amazon Inspector Agent on multiple EC2 instances using the Systems Manager Run Command
- To install the Amazon Inspector Agent on a Linux-based EC2 instance
- To install the Amazon Inspector Agent on a Windows-based EC2 instance

Note
The following procedures are functional in all regions that are supported by Amazon Inspector.

Amazon Linux AMI with Amazon Inspector Agent

To skip the manual Amazon Inspector Agent installation on the Amazon Linux EC2 instances that you want to include in your assessment targets, you can use the ** Amazon Linux AMI with Amazon Inspector Agent**. This AMI has the Amazon Inspector Agent pre-installed and requires no additional steps to install or setup the agent. To start using Amazon Inspector with these EC2 instances, simply tag them to match the desired assessment target. The configuration of ** Amazon Linux AMI with Amazon Inspector Agent** enhances security by focusing on two main security goals: limiting access and reducing software vulnerabilities.

This is the only currently available EC2 instance AMI with the pre-installed Amazon Inspector Agent. For the EC2 instances running Ubuntu Server or Windows Server, you must complete the manual Amazon Inspector Agent installation steps.

The ** Amazon Linux AMI with Amazon Inspector Agent** is available in the EC2 console and also the AWS Marketplace.

To install the Amazon Inspector Agent on multiple EC2 instances using the Systems Manager Run Command

You can install the Amazon Inspector Agent on your EC2 instances using the Systems Manager Run Command. This enables you to install the agent remotely and on multiple instances (both Linux-based and Windows-based instances with the same command) at once.

Important
Agent installation using the Systems Manager Run Command is not currently supported for the Debian operating system.

Important
To utilize this option, make sure that your EC2 instance has the SSM Agent installed and has an IAM role that allows Run Command. The SSM Agent is installed, by default, on Amazon EC2 Windows instances and Amazon Linux instances. Amazon EC2 Systems Manager requires an IAM role for EC2 instances that will process commands and a separate role for users executing commands. For more information, see Installing and Configuring SSM Agent and Configuring Security Roles for System Manager.

1. Open the Amazon EC2 console at https://console.aws.amazon.com/ec2/.

2. In the navigation pane under **Systems Manager Services**, choose **Run Command**.

3. Choose **Run a command**.

4. For **Command document**, choose the document named

   AmazonInspector-ManageAWSAgent owned by **Amazon**. This document contains the script for installing the Amazon Inspector Agent on EC2 instances.

5. Specify your EC2 instances either by choosing the **Specifying a Tag** option or by **Manually Selecting Instances** and then selecting **Select instances**. To install the agent on all the instances in the assessment target, you can specify the same tags used for creating the assessment target.

6. Provide your choices for the rest of the available options using the instructions in Executing Commands from the EC2 Console, and then select **Run**.

Note
You can also install the Amazon Inspector Agent on multiple EC2 instances (both Linux-based and Windows-based) while creating a new assessment target or by using the **Install Agents with Run Command** button for an existing target. For more information, see Creating an Assessment Target (Console).

To install the Amazon Inspector Agent on a Linux-based EC2 instance

1. Sign in to your EC2 instance running a Linux-based operating system where you want to install the Amazon Inspector Agent. **Note**
   For more information about operating systems supported for Amazon Inspector see Amazon Inspector Supported Operating Systems and Regions.

2. Download the agent installation script by running one of the following commands:

   - wget https://d1wk0tztpsntt1/.cloudfront/.net/linux/latest/install
   - curl -O https://d1wk0tztpsntt1/.cloudfront/.net/linux/latest/install

3. (Optional) Verify that the Amazon Inspector Agent installation script is not altered or corrupted. For more information, see (Optional) Verify the Signature of the Amazon Inspector Agent Installation Script on Linux-based Operating Systems.

4. To install the agent, run sudo bash install. **Note**
   As updates for the Amazon Inspector Agent become available, they are automatically downloaded from Amazon S3 and applied. For more information, see Amazon Inspector Agent Updates.
   If you want to skip this auto-update process, make sure to run the following command when you install the agent:
   sudo bash install -u false **Note**
   (Optional) To remove the agent installation script, run rm install .

5. Verify that the following files required for the agent to be successfully installed and functioning properly are installed:

   - libcurl4 (required to install the agent on Ubuntu 18.04)
   - libcurl3
   - libgcc1
   - libc6
   - libstdc++6
   - libssl1.0.1
   - libssl1.0.2 (required to install the agent on Debian 9)
   - libpcap0.8

To install the Amazon Inspector Agent on a Windows-based EC2 instance

1. Sign in to your EC2 instance running a Windows-based operating system where you want to install the Amazon Inspector Agent. **Note**

For more information about operating systems supported for Amazon Inspector see Amazon Inspector Supported Operating Systems and Regions.

2. Download the following .exe file: https://d1wk0tztpsntt1/.cloudfront/.net/windows/installer/latest/ AWSAgentInstall/.exe

3. Open a command prompt window (with Administrative permissions), navigate to the location where you saved the downloaded AWSAgentInstall.exe, and run AWSAgentInstall.exe to install the Amazon Inspector Agent. **Note**
As updates for the Amazon Inspector Agent become available, they are automatically downloaded from Amazon S3 and applied. For more information, see Amazon Inspector Agent Updates.
If you want to skip this auto-update process, make sure to run this command to install the Amazon Inspector Agent.
AWSAgentInstall.exe AUTOUPDATE=No

Working with Amazon Inspector Agents on Linux-based Operating Systems

Sign in to your EC2 instance running a Linux-based operating system, and run any of the following procedures. For more information about operating systems supported for Amazon Inspector see Amazon Inspector Supported Operating Systems and Regions.

Note
The following commands are functional in all regions that are supported by Amazon Inspector.

Topics

- To verify that the Amazon Inspector Agent is running
- To stop the Amazon Inspector Agent
- To start the Amazon Inspector Agent
- To configure proxy support for Amazon Inspector Agents
- To uninstall the Amazon Inspector Agent

To verify that the Amazon Inspector Agent is running

- To verify that the Amazon Inspector Agent is installed and running, sign in to your EC2 instance, and run the following command:

  sudo /opt/aws/awsagent/bin/awsagent status

  This command returns the status of the currently running agent, or an error stating that the agent cannot be contacted.

To stop the Amazon Inspector Agent

- To stop the agent, run sudo /etc/init.d/awsagent stop

To start the Amazon Inspector Agent

- To start the agent, run sudo /etc/init.d/awsagent start

To configure proxy support for Amazon Inspector Agents

Proxy support for Amazon Inspector Agents on Linux-based operating systems is achieved by using an Amazon Inspector Agent specific configuration file with specific environment variables. For more information, see https://wiki.archlinux.org/index.php/proxy_settings.

Complete one of the following procedures:

To install an Amazon Inspector Agent on an EC2 instance that uses a proxy server

1. Create a file called `awsagent.env` and save it in the `/etc/init.d/` directory.

2. Edit awsagent.env to include these environment variables in the following format:

   - export https_proxy=hostname:port
   - export http_proxy=hostname:port
   - export no_proxy=169.254.169.254 **Note**
     Substitute example values above with valid hostname and port number combinations only. You must specify the IP address of the instance metadata endpoint (169.254.169.254) for the `no_proxy` variable.

3. Install the Amazon Inspector Agent by completing the steps in the To install the Amazon Inspector Agent on a Linux-based EC2 instance procedure.

To configure proxy support on an EC2 instance with a running Amazon Inspector Agent

1. In order to configure proxy support, the version of the Amazon Inspector Agent that is running on your EC2 instance must be 1.0.800.1 or higher. If you have the auto-update process for the Amazon Inspector Agent enabled, you can verify that your Amazon Inspector Agent's version is 1.0.800.1 or higher by using the To verify that the Amazon Inspector Agent is running procedure. If you don't have the auto-update process for the Amazon Inspector Agent enabled, you must install the agent on this EC2 instance again by following the To install the Amazon Inspector Agent on a Linux-based EC2 instance procedure.

2. Create a file called `awsagent.env` and save it in the `/etc/init.d/` directory.

3. Edit awsagent.env to include these environment variables in the following format:

   - export https_proxy=hostname:port
   - export http_proxy=hostname:port
   - export no_proxy=169.254.169.254 **Note**
     Substitute example values above with valid hostname and port number combinations only. You must specify the IP address of the instance metadata endpoint (169.254.169.254) for the `no_proxy` variable.

4. Restart the Amazon Inspector Agent by first stopping it using `sudo /etc/init.d/awsagent restart`.

   Proxy settings are picked up and used by both the Amazon Inspector Agent and the auto-update process.

To uninstall the Amazon Inspector Agent

1. Sign in to your EC2 instance running a Linux-based operating system where you want to uninstall the Amazon Inspector Agent. **Note**
   For more information about operating systems supported for Amazon Inspector see Amazon Inspector Supported Operating Systems and Regions.

2. To uninstall the agent, use one of the following commands:

   - On Amazon Linux, CentOS, and Red Hat, run sudo yum remove 'AwsAgent*'
   - On Ubuntu Server, run sudo apt-get purge 'awsagent*'

Working with Amazon Inspector Agents on Windows-based Operating Systems

Sign in to your EC2 instance running a Windows-based operating system and run any of the following procedures. For more information about operating systems supported for Amazon Inspector see Amazon Inspector Supported Operating Systems and Regions.

Note
The following commands are functional in all regions that are supported by Amazon Inspector.

Topics
- To stop or start the Amazon Inspector Agent or verify that the Amazon Inspector Agent is running
- To modify Amazon Inspector Agent settings
- To configure proxy support for Amazon Inspector Agents
- To uninstall the Amazon Inspector Agent

To stop or start the Amazon Inspector Agent or verify that the Amazon Inspector Agent is running

1. On your EC2 instance, choose **Start**, then **Run**, and then type **services.msc**.

2. If the agent is successfully running, two services are listed with their status set to **Started** or **Running** in the Services Window: **AWS Agent Service** and **AWS Agent Updater Service**.

3. To start the agent, right-click **AWS Agent Service** and then choose **Start**. If the service is successfully started, the status is updated to **Started** or **Running**.

4. To stop the agent, right-click **AWS Agent Service** and choose **Stop**. If the service is successfully stopped, the status is cleared (appears as blank). We do not recommend stopping the **AWS Agent Updater Service** as it will disable the installation of all future enhancements and fixes to the Amazon Inspector Agent.

5. To verify that the Amazon Inspector Agent is installed and running, sign in to your EC2 instance, open a command prompt with Administrative permissions, navigate to C:/Program Files/Amazon Web Services/AWS Agent, and then run the following command:

   AWSAgentStatus.exe

   This command returns the status of the currently running agent, or an error stating that the agent cannot be contacted.

To modify Amazon Inspector Agent settings

Once the Amazon Inspector Agent is installed and running on your EC2 instance, you can modify the settings in the **agent.cfg file** to alter the agent's behavior. The **agent.cfg** file is located in the **/opt/aws/awsagent/etc** directory on Linux-based operating systems and in the **C:\ProgramData\Amazon Web Services\AWS Agent** directory on Windows-based operating systems After you modify and save the **agent.cfg file**, you must stop and start the agent in order for the changes to take effect.

Important
We highly recommend that you modify the **agent.cfg** file only with the guidance of AWS Support.

To configure proxy support for Amazon Inspector Agents

Proxy support for Amazon Inspector Agents is achieved through the use of the WinHTTP proxy. To set up WinHTTP proxy using the `netsh` utility see: https://technet.microsoft.com/en-us/library/cc731131%28v=ws.10%29.aspx.

Complete one of the following procedures:

To install an Amazon Inspector Agent on an EC2 instance that uses a proxy server

1. Download the following .exe file: `https://d1wk0tztpsntt1.cloudfront.net/windows/installer/latest/AWSAgentInstall.exe`

2. Open a command prompt window or PowerShell window (with Administrative permissions), navigate to the location where you saved the downloaded AWSAgentInstall.exe, and run the following command:

   `./AWSAgentInstall.exe \install USEPROXY=1`

To configure proxy support on an EC2 instance with a running Amazon Inspector Agent

1. In order to configure proxy support, the version of the Amazon Inspector Agent that is running on your EC2 instance must be 1.0.0.59 or higher. If you have the auto-update process for the Amazon Inspector Agent enabled, you can verify that your Amazon Inspector Agent's version is 1.0.0.59 or higher by using the To stop or start the Amazon Inspector Agent or verify that the Amazon Inspector Agent is running procedure. If you don't have the auto-update process for the Amazon Inspector Agent enabled, you must install the agent on this EC2 instance again by following the To install the Amazon Inspector Agent on a Windows-based EC2 instance procedure.

2. Open the registry editor (regedit.exe).

3. Navigate to the following Registry key "`HKEY_LOCAL_MACHINE/SOFTWARE/Amazon Web Services/AWS Agent Updater`".

4. Inside this registry key, create a registry DWORD(32bit) value called "`UseProxy`".

5. Double click on the value and set the value to 1.

6. Type `services.msc`, locate the **AWS Agent Service** and the **AWS Agent Updater Service** in the Services Window, and restart each process. After both processes have successfully restarted, run `AWSAgentStatus.exe` (see Step 5 in To stop or start the Amazon Inspector Agent or verify that the Amazon Inspector Agent is running) to view the status of your Amazon Inspector Agent and verify that it is using the configured proxy.

To uninstall the Amazon Inspector Agent

1. Sign in to your EC2 instance running a Windows-based operating system where you want to uninstall the Amazon Inspector Agent. **Note**
   For more information about operating systems supported for Amazon Inspector see Amazon Inspector Supported Operating Systems and Regions.

2. On your EC2 instance, navigate to **Control Panel, Add/Remove Programs.**

3. In the list of installed programs, choose **AWS Agent**, and then choose **Uninstall**.

(Optional) Verify the Signature of the Amazon Inspector Agent Installation Script on Linux-based Operating Systems

This topic describes the recommended process of verifying the validity of the Amazon Inspector Agent's installations script for Linux-based operating systems.

Whenever you download an application from the Internet, we recommend that you authenticate the identity of the software publisher and check that the application is not altered or corrupted since it was published. This protects you from installing a version of the application that contains a virus or other malicious code.

If after running the steps in this topic, you determine that the software for the Amazon Inspector Agent is altered or corrupted, do NOT run the installation file. Instead, contact Amazon Web Services.

Amazon Inspector Agent files for Linux-based operating systems are signed using GnuPG, an open source implementation of the Pretty Good Privacy (OpenPGP) standard for secure digital signatures. GnuPG (also known as GPG) provides authentication and integrity checking through a digital signature. Amazon EC2 publishes a public key and signatures that you can use to verify the downloaded Amazon EC2 CLI tools. For more information about PGP and GnuPG (GPG), see http://www.gnupg.org.

The first step is to establish trust with the software publisher: Download the public key of the software publisher, check that the owner of the public key is who they claim to be, and then add the public key to your *keyring*. Your keyring is a collection of known public keys. After you establish the authenticity of the public key, you can use it to verify the signature of the application.

Topics

- Install the GPG Tools
- Authenticate and Import the Public Key
- Verify the Signature of the Package

Install the GPG Tools

If your operating system is Linux or Unix, the GPG tools are likely already installed. To test whether the tools are installed on your system, type gpg at a command prompt. If the GPG tools are installed, you see a GPG command prompt. If the GPG tools are not installed, you see an error stating that the command cannot be found. You can install the GnuPG package from a repository.

To install GPG tools on Debian-based Linux

- From a terminal, run the following command: apt-get install gnupg.

To install GPG tools on Red Hat–based Linux

- From a terminal, run the following command: yum install gnupg.

Authenticate and Import the Public Key

The next step in the process is to authenticate the Amazon Inspector public key and add it as a trusted key in your GPG keyring.

To authenticate and import the Amazon Inspector public key

1. Obtain a copy of our public GPG build key by doing one of the following:

    - Download from https://d1wk0tztpsntt1.cloudfront.net/linux/latest/inspector.gpg.

    - Copy the key from the following text and paste it into a file called `inspector.key`. Be sure to include everything that follows:

```
1 -----BEGIN PGP PUBLIC KEY BLOCK-----
2 Version: GnuPG v2.0.18 (GNU/Linux)
3
4 mQINBFYDlfEBEADFpfNt/mdCtsmfDoga+PfHY9bdXAD68yhp2m9NyH3BOzle/MXI
5 8siNfoRgzDwuWnIaezHwwLWkDw2paRxp1NMQ9qRe8Phq0ewheLrQu95dwDgMcw90
6 gf9m1iKVHjdVQ9qNHlB2OFknPDxMDRHcrmlJYDKYCX3+MODEHnlK25tIH2KWezXP
7 FPSU+TkwjLRzSMYH1L8IwjFUIIi78jQS9a31R/cOl4zuC5fOVghYlSomLI8irfoD
8 JSa3csVRujSmOAf9o3beiMR/kNDMpgDOxgiQTu/Kh39cl6o8AKe+QKK48kqO7hra
9 h1dpzLbfeZEVU6dWMZtlUksG/zKxuzD6d8vXYH7Z+x09POPFALQCQQMC3WisIKgj
10 zJEFhXMCCQ3NLC3CeyMq3vP7MbVRBYE7t3d2uDREkZBgIf+mbUYfYPhrzy0qT9Tr
11 PgwcnUvDZuazxuuPzucZGOJ5kbptat3DcUpstjdkMGAId3JawBbps77qRZdA+swr
12 o9o3jbowgmf0y5ZS6KwvZnC6XyTAkXy2io7mSrAIRECrANrzYzfp5v7uD7w8Dk0X
13 1OrfOm1VufMzAyTu0YQGBWaQKzSB8tCkvFw54PrRuUTcV826XU7SIJNzmNQo58uL
14 bKyLVBSCVabfs0lkECIesq8PT9xMYfQJ421uATHyYUnFTU2TYrCQEab7oQARAQAB
15 tCdBbWF6b24gSW5zcGVjdG9yIDxpbnNwZWN0b3JAYW1hem9uLmNvbT6JAjgEEwEC
16 ACIFAlYDlfECGwMGCwkIBwMCBhUIAgkKCwQWAgMBAh4BAheAAAoJECROCWBYNgQY
17 8yUP/2GpIl40f3mKBUiSTe0XQLvwiBCHmY+V9fOuKqDTinxssjEMCnz0vsKeCZF/
18 L35pwNa/oW0OJa8D7sCkKG+8LuyMpcPDyqptLrYPprUWtz2+qLCHgpWsrku7ateF
19 x4hWS0jUVeHPaBzI9V1NTHsCx9+nbpWQ5Fk+7VJI8hbMDY7NQx6fcse8WTlP/0r/
20 HIkKzzqQQaaOf5t9zc5DKwi+dFmJbRUyaq22xs8C81UODjHunhjHdZ21cnsgk91S
21 fviuaum9aR4/uVIYOTVWnjC5J3+VlczyUt5FaYrrQ5ov0dM+biTUXwve3X8Q85Nu
22 DPnO/+zxb7Jz3QCHXnuTbxZTjvvl60Oi8//uRTnPXjz4wZLwQfibgHmk1++hzND7
23 wOYA02Js6v5FZQlLQAod7q2wuA1pq4MroLXzziDfy/9ea8B+tzyxlmNVRpVZY4Ll
24 DOHyqGQhpkyV3drjjNZlEofwbfu7m6ODwsgM15ynzhKklJzwPJFfB3mMc7qLi+qX
25 MJtEX8KJ/iVUQStHHAG7daL1bxpWSI3BRuaHsWbBGQ/mcHBgUUOQJyEp5LAdg9Fs
26 VP55gWtF7pIqifiqlcfgGOOv+A3NmVbmiGKSZvfrc5KsF/k43rCGqDx1RV6gZvyI
27 Lf09+3sEIlNrsMibOKRLDeBt3EuDsaBZgOkqjDhgJUesqiCy
28 =iEhB
29 -----END PGP PUBLIC KEY BLOCK-----
```

2. At a command prompt in the directory where you saved **inspector.key**, use the following command to import the Amazon Inspector public key into your keyring:

```
1 gpg --import inspector.key
```

The command returns results similar to the following:

```
1 gpg: key 58360418: public key "Amazon Inspector <inspector@amazon.com>" imported
2                  gpg: Total number processed: 1
3                  gpg:                      imported: 1  (RSA: 1)
```

Make a note of the key value; you need it in the next step. In the preceding example, the key value is 58360418

3. Verify the fingerprint by running the following command, replacing *key-value* with the value from the preceding step:

```
1 gpg --fingerprint key-value
```

This command returns results similar to the following:

```
1 pub    4096R/58360418 2015-09-24
2                Key fingerprint = DDA0 D4C5 10AE 3C20 6F46  6DC0 2474 0960 5836 0418
3                uid                      Amazon Inspector <inspector@amazon.com>
```

Additionally, the fingerprint string should be identical to DDA0 D4C5 10AE 3C20 6F46 6DC0 2474 0960 5836 0418 as shown above. Compare the key fingerprint returned to that published on this page. They should match. If they do not match, do not install the Amazon Inspector Agent installation script, and contact Amazon Web Services.

Verify the Signature of the Package

After you've installed the GPG tools, authenticated and imported the Amazon Inspector public key, and verified that the Amazon Inspector public key is trusted, you are ready to verify the signature of the Amazon Inspector installation script.

To verify the Amazon Inspector installation script signature

1. At a command prompt, run the following command to download the signature file for the installation script:

```
1 curl -O https://d1wk0tztpsntt1.cloudfront.net/linux/latest/install.sig
```

2. Verify the signature by running the following command at a command prompt in the directory where you saved `install.sig` and the Amazon Inspector installation file. Both files must be present.

```
1 gpg --verify ./install.sig
```

The output should look something like the following:

```
1 gpg: Signature made Thu 24 Sep 2015 03:19:09 PM UTC using RSA key ID 58360418
2 gpg: Good signature from "Amazon Inspector <inspector@amazon.com>" [unknown]
3 gpg: WARNING: This key is not certified with a trusted signature!
4 gpg:          There is no indication that the signature belongs to the owner.
5 Primary key fingerprint: DDA0 D4C5 10AE 3C20 6F46  6DC0 2474 0960 5836 0418
```

If the output contains the phrase `Good signature from "Amazon Inspector <inspector@amazon.com>"`, it means that the signature has successfully been verified, and you can proceed to run the Amazon Inspector installation script.

If the output includes the phrase `BAD signature`, check whether you performed the procedure correctly. If you continue to get this response, contact Amazon Web Services and do not run the installation file that you downloaded previously.

The following are details about the warnings you might see:

- **WARNING: This key is not certified with a trusted signature! There is no indication that the signature belongs to the owner. **This refers to your personal level of trust in your belief that you possess an authentic public key for Amazon Inspector. In an ideal world, you would visit an Amazon Web Services office and receive the key in person. However, more often you download it from a website. In this case, the website is an Amazon Web Services web site.
- **gpg: no ultimately trusted keys found.** This means that the specific key is not "ultimately trusted" by you (or by other people whom you trust).

For more information, see http://www.gnupg.org.

(Optional) Verify the Signature of the Amazon Inspector Agent Installation Script on Windows-based Operating Systems

This topic describes the recommended process of verifying the validity of the Amazon Inspector Agent's installations script for Windows-based operating systems.

Whenever you download an application from the Internet, we recommend that you authenticate the identity of the software publisher and check that the application is not altered or corrupted since it was published. This protects you from installing a version of the application that contains a virus or other malicious code.

If after running the steps in this topic, you determine that the software for the Amazon Inspector Agent is altered or corrupted, do NOT run the installation file. Instead, contact Amazon Web Services.

To verify the validity of the downloaded Amazon Inspector Agent installation script on Windows-based operating systems, you must make sure that the thumbprint of its Amazon Services LLC signer certificate is equal to this value:

5C 2C B5 5A 9A B9 B1 D6 3F F4 1B 0D A2 76 F2 A9 2B 09 A8 6A

To verify this value, perform the following procedure:

1. Right-click the downloaded `AWSAgentInstall.exe` and open the **Properties** window.

2. Choose the **Digital Signatures** tab.

3. From the **Signature List**, choose **Amazon Services LLC**, and then choose **Details**.

4. Choose the **General** tab, if not already selected, and then choose **View Certificate**.

5. Choose the **Details** tab and then choose **All** in the **Show:** dropdown list, if not already selected.

6. Scroll down until you see the **Thumbprint** field and then choose **Thumbprint**. This will display the entire thumbprint value in the lower window.

   - If the thumbprint value in the lower window is identical to the following value:

     5C 2C B5 5A 9A B9 B1 D6 3F F4 1B 0D A2 76 F2 A9 2B 09 A8 6A

     then your downloaded Amazon Inspector Agent installation script is authentic and can be safely installed.

   - If the thumbprint value in the lower details window is NOT identical to the value above, do NOT run `AWSAgentInstall.exe`.

Amazon Inspector Assessment Targets

You can use Amazon Inspector to evaluate whether your AWS assessment targets (your collections of AWS resources) have potential security issues that you need to address.

Important
In this release of Amazon Inspector, your assessment targets can consist only of EC2 instances that run on a number of supported operating systems. For more information about supported Linux-based and Windows-based operating systems, and supported AWS regions, see Amazon Inspector Service Limits.

Note
For more information about launching EC2 instances, see Amazon Elastic Compute Cloud Documentation.

Topics

- Tagging Resources to Create an Assessment Target
- Amazon Inspector Assessment Targets Limits
- Creating an Assessment Target (Console)
- Deleting an Assessment Target (Console)

Tagging Resources to Create an Assessment Target

To create an assessment target for Amazon Inspector to assess, you start by tagging the EC2 instances that you want to include in your target. Tags are words or phrases that act as metadata for identifying and organizing your instances and other AWS resources. Amazon Inspector uses the tags that you create to identify the instances that belong to your target.

Every AWS tag consists of a key and value pair of your choice. For example, you might choose to name your key "Name" and your value "MyFirstInstance". After you tag your instances, you use the Amazon Inspector console to add the instances to your assessment target. It is not necessary that any instance match more than one tag key-value pair.

When you tag your EC2 instances to build assessment targets for Amazon Inspector to assess, you can create your own custom tag keys or use tag keys created by others in the same AWS account. You also can use the tag keys that AWS automatically creates, for example, the **Name** tag key that is automatically created for the EC2 instances that you launch.

You can add tags to EC2 instances when you create them or add, change, or remove those tags one at a time within each EC2 instance's console page. You can also add tags to multiple EC2 instances at once using the Tag Editor.

For more information, see Tag Editor. For more information about tagging EC2 instances, see Resources and Tags.

Amazon Inspector Assessment Targets Limits

You can create up to 50 assessment targets per AWS account. For more information, see Amazon Inspector Service Limits.

Creating an Assessment Target (Console)

You can use the Amazon Inspector console to create assessment targets.

To create an assessment target

1. Sign in to the AWS Management Console and open the Amazon Inspector console at https://console.aws. amazon.com/inspector/.

2. In the navigation pane, choose **Assessment Targets**, and then choose **Create**.

3. For **Name**, type a name for your assessment target.

4. Do one of the following:

   - Check the **All instances** checkbox to include all EC2 instances in this AWS account and region in this assessment target. **Note**
     The limit on the maximum number of agents that can be included in an assessment run applies when you use this option. For more information, see Amazon Inspector Service Limits.
   - Use the **Tags' Key** and **Value** fields to type the tag key name and key-value pairs in order to select the EC2 instances that you want to include in this assessment target.

5. (Optional) While creating a new target, you can check the checkbox to install the Amazon Inspector Agent on all EC2 instances in this target. To use this option, your EC2 instances must have the SSM Agent installed and an IAM role that allows Run Command. The SSM Agent is installed, by default, on Amazon EC2 Windows instances and Amazon Linux instances. Amazon EC2 Systems Manager requires an IAM role for EC2 instances that will process commands and a separate role for users executing commands. For more information, see Installing and Configuring SSM Agent and Configuring Security Roles for System Manager. **Important**
   If an EC2 instance already has an agent running on it, using this option replaces the agent currently running on the instance with the latest agent version. **Note**
   For your existing assessment targets, you can select the **Install Agents with Run Command button** to install the Amazon Inspector Agent on all EC2 instances in this target. **Note**
   You can also install the Amazon Inspector Agent on multiple EC2 instances (both Linux-based and Windows-based instances with the same command) remotely by using the Systems Manager Run Command. For more information, see To install the Amazon Inspector Agent on multiple EC2 instances using the Systems Manager Run Command.

6. Choose **Save**.

Note
For your existing assessment targets, you can use the **Preview Target** button on the **Assessment Targets** page to review all EC2 instances that are currently included in the assessment targets. For every EC2 instance listed, you can review the hostname, instance ID, IP address, and the status of the Amazon Inspector Agent that is running on the EC2 instance. The agent status can have the following values: **HEALTHY, UNHEALTHY** (displayed when the agent is reporting that it is not in a healthy state), and **UNKNOWN** (displayed when Amazon Inspector is unable to determine whether there is an Amazon Inspector Agent running on the EC2 instance).

Deleting an Assessment Target (Console)

To delete an assessment target, perform the following procedure:

- In the **Assessment targets** page, choose the target you want to delete, and then choose **Delete**. When prompted for confirmation, choose **Yes. Important**
  When you delete an assessment target, all assessment templates, assessment runs, findings and versions of the reports associated with the target are also deleted.

You can also delete an assessment target by using the DeleteAssessmentTarget API.

Amazon Inspector Assessment Templates and Assessment Runs

Amazon Inspector helps you discover potential security issues by using security rules to analyze your AWS resources. Amazon Inspector monitors and collects behavioral data (telemetry) about your resources, such as the use of secure channels, network traffic among running processes, and details of communication with AWS services. Next, Amazon Inspector analyzes and compares the data against a set of security rules packages. Finally, Amazon Inspector produces a list of *findings* that identify potential security issues of various severity.

To get started, you create an *assessment target* (a collection of the AWS resources that you want Amazon Inspector to analyze) and an *assessment template* (a blueprint that you use to configure your assessment). You use the template to start an *assessment run*, the monitoring and analysis process that results in a set of findings.

Topics

- Amazon Inspector Assessment Templates
- Amazon Inspector Assessment Templates Limits
- Creating an Assessment Template (Console)
- Deleting an Assessment Template (Console)
- Assessment Runs
- Amazon Inspector Assessment Runs Limits
- Setting Up Automatic Assessment Runs Through a Lambda Function
- Setting Up an SNS Topic for Amazon Inspector Notifications (Console)

Amazon Inspector Assessment Templates

An assessment template allows you to specify a configuration for your assessment runs, including the following:

- Rules packages that Amazon Inspector uses to evaluate your assessment target
- Duration of the assessment run **Note**
  You can set your duration to any of the following available values:
  15 minutes 1 hour (recommended) 8 hours 12 hours 24 hours The longer your running assessment template's duration is, the more thorough and complete is the set of telemetry that Amazon Inspector can collect and analyze. In other words, longer analysis allows Amazon Inspector to observe the behavior of your assessment target in greater detail and to produce fuller sets of findings. Similarly, the more thoroughly you use your AWS resources that are included in your target during the assessment run, the more thorough and complete is the telemetry set that Amazon Inspector collects and analyzes.
- Amazon Simple Notification Service (SNS) topics to which you want Amazon Inspector to send notifications about assessment run states and findings
- Amazon Inspector-specific attributes (key-value pairs) that you can assign to findings that are generated by the assessment run that uses this assessment template

After Amazon Inspector creates the assessment template, you can tag it like any other AWS resource. For more information, see Tag Editor. Tagging assessment templates enables you to organize them and get better oversight of your security strategy. For example, Amazon Inspector offers a large number of rules that you can assess your assessment targets against, but you might want to include various subsets of the available rules in your assessment templates in order to target specific areas of concern or to uncover specific security problems. Tagging assessment templates allows you to locate and run them quickly at any time in accordance with your security strategy and goals.

Important
After you create an assessment template, you can't modify it.

Amazon Inspector Assessment Templates Limits

You can create up to 500 assessment templates per AWS account.

For more information, see Amazon Inspector Service Limits.

Creating an Assessment Template (Console)

1. Sign in to the AWS Management Console and open the Amazon Inspector console at https://console.aws.amazon.com/inspector/.

2. From the navigation pane on the left, choose **Assessment Templates**, and then choose **Create**.

3. For **Name**, type a name for your assessment template.

4. For **Target name**, choose an assessment target to analyze. **Note**
   While in the process of creating a new assessment template, you can use the **Preview Target** button on the **Assessment Templates** page to review all EC2 instances that are currently included in the assessment target that you want to include in this template. For every EC2 instance listed, you can review the hostname, instance ID, IP address, and the status of the Amazon Inspector Agent that is running on the EC2 instance. The agent status can have the following values: **HEALTHY**, **UNHEALTHY** (displayed when the agent is reporting that it is not in a healthy state), and **UNKNOWN** (displayed when Amazon Inspector is unable to determine whether there is an Amazon Inspector Agent running on the EC2 instance).
   You can also use the **Preview Target** button on the **Assessment Templates** page to review EC2 instances that make up assessment targets included in your previously created templates.

5. For **Rules packages**, choose one or more rules packages to include in your assessment template.

6. For **Duration**, specify the duration for your assessment template.

7. For **SNS topics**, specify an SNS topic to which you want Amazon Inspector to send notifications about assessment run states and findings. Amazon Inspector can send SNS notifications about the following events:

   - An assessment run has started
   - An assessment run has ended
   - An assessment run's status has changed
   - A finding was generated

   For more information about setting up an SNS topic to which Amazon Inspector can send notifications, see Setting Up an SNS Topic for Amazon Inspector Notifications (Console).

8. (Optional) For **Tag**, type values for **Key** and **Value**. You can add multiple tags to the assessment template.

9. (Optional) For **Attributes added to findings**, type values for **Key** and **Value**. Amazon Inspector applies the attributes to all findings generated by the assessment template. You can add multiple attributes to the assessment template. For more information about findings and tagging findings, see Amazon Inspector Findings.

10. (Optional) To set up a schedule for your assessment runs using this template, you can check the **Set up recurring assessment runs once every <number_of_days>, starting now** checkbox and specify the recurrence pattern (number of days) using the up and down arrows. **Note**
    When you use this checkbox, Amazon Inspector automatically creates a CloudWatch Events rule for the assessment runs schedule that you are setting up. Amazon Inspector then also automatically creates an IAM role named AWS_InspectorEvents_Invoke_Assessment_Template. This role enables CloudWatch Events to make API calls against the Amazon Inspector resources. For more information, see What is Amazon CloudWatch Events? and Using Resource-Based Policies for CloudWatch Events. **Note**
    You can also set up automatic assessment runs through a Lambda function. For more information, see Setting Up Automatic Assessment Runs Through a Lambda Function.

11. Choose **Create and run** or **Create**.

Deleting an Assessment Template (Console)

To delete an assessment template, perform the following procedure:

- In the **Assessment Templates** page, choose the template you want to delete, and then choose **Delete**. When prompted for confirmation, choose **Yes. Important**
  When you delete an assessment template, all assessment runs, findings, and versions of the reports associated with this template are also deleted.

You can also delete an assessment template by using the DeleteAssessmentTemplate API.

Assessment Runs

After you create an assessment template, you can use it to start assessment runs. You can start multiple assessment runs using the same template as long as you stay within the assessment runs limit per AWS account. For more information, see Amazon Inspector Assessment Runs Limits .

If you use the Amazon Inspector console, you must start the first run of your new assessment template from the **Assessment templates** page. After you start the run, you can use the **Assessment runs** page to monitor the run's progress. Use the **Run**, **Cancel**, and **Delete** buttons to start, cancel, or delete a run. Use the XYZ widget next to the run's **Start time** to view the run's details, including the ARN of the run, the rules packages selected for the run, the tags and attributes that you applied to the run, and more.

For subsequent runs of the assessment template, you can use the **Run**, **Cancel**, and **Delete** buttons on either the **Assessment templates** page or the **Assessment runs** page.

Deleting an Assessment Run (Console)

To delete an assessment run, perform the following procedure:

- In the **Assessment runs** page, choose the run you want to delete, and then choose **Delete**. When prompted for confirmation, choose **Yes. Important**
  When you delete an assessment run, all findings and all versions of the report from that run are also deleted.

You can also delete an assessment run by using the DeleteAssessmentRun API.

Amazon Inspector Assessment Runs Limits

You can create up to 50,000 assessment runs per AWS account.

You can have multiple assessment runs happening at the same time as long as the assessment targets used for these runs do not contain overlapping EC2 instances.

For more information, see Amazon Inspector Service Limits.

Setting Up Automatic Assessment Runs Through a Lambda Function

If you want to set up a recurring schedule for your assessment, you can configure your assessment template to run automatically by creating a Lambda function through the AWS Lambda console. For more information, see Lambda Functions.

To set up automatic assessment runs using the AWS Lambda console, perform the following procedure:

1. Sign in to the AWS Management Console, and open the AWS Lambda console.

2. From the navigation pane on the left, choose either **Dashboard** or **Functions**, and then choose **Create a Lambda Function**.

3. On the **Select blueprint** page, choose the **inspector-scheduled-run** blueprint. You can find this blueprint by typing **inspector** in the **Filter** field.

4. On the **Configure triggers** page, set up a recurring schedule for automated assessment runs by specifying a CloudWatch event that triggers your function. To do this, type a rule name and description, and then choose a schedule expression. The schedule expression determines how often the run will occur, for example, every 15 minutes or once a day. For more information about CloudWatch events and concepts, see What is Amazon CloudWatch Events?

   If you select the **Enable trigger** check box, the assessment run begins immediately after you finish creating your function. Subsequent automated runs will follow the recurrence pattern that you specify in the **Schedule expression** field. If you don't select the **Enable trigger** check box while creating the function, you can edit the function later to enable this trigger.

5. On the **Configure function** page, specify the following:

   - For **Name**, type a name for your function.

   - (Optional) For **Description**, type a description that will help you identify your function later.

   - For **runtime**, keep the default value of **Node.js 4.3**. AWS Lambda supports the **inspector-scheduled-run** blueprint only for the **Node.js 4.3** runtime.

   - The assessment template that you want to run automatically using this function. You do this by providing the value for the environment variable called **assessmentTemplateArn**.

   - Keep the handler set to the default value of **index.handler**.

   - The permissions for your function using the **Role** field. For more information, see AWS Lambda Permissions Model.

     To run this function, you need an IAM role that allows AWS Lambda to start assessment runs and write log messages about assessment runs, including any errors, to Amazon CloudWatch logs. AWS Lambda assumes this role for every recurring automated assessment run. For example, you can attach the following sample policy to this IAM role:

```
{
  "Version": "2012-10-17",
  "Statement": [
    {
      "Effect": "Allow",
      "Action": [
        "inspector:StartAssessmentRun",
        "logs:CreateLogGroup",
        "logs:CreateLogStream",
        "logs:PutLogEvents"
      ],
      "Resource": "*"
    }
  ]
}
```

6. Review your selections, and then choose **Create function**.

Setting Up an SNS Topic for Amazon Inspector Notifications (Console)

Amazon Simple Notification Service (Amazon SNS) is a web service that sends messages to subscribing endpoints or clients. You can use Amazon SNS to set up notifications for Amazon Inspector. For more information, see What is Amazon Simple Notification Service?.

To set up an SNS topic for notifications

1. Create an SNS topic. For more information, see Create a Topic.

2. Subscribe to the SNS topic that you created. For more information, see Subscribe to a Topic.

3. Publish to the SNS topic. For more information, see Publish to a Topic.

4. Enable Amazon Inspector to publish messages to the topic:

    1. Open the Amazon SNS console at https://console.aws.amazon.com/sns/.

    2. Select your SNS topic, and for **Actions**, choose **Edit topic policy**.

    3. For **Allow these users to publish messages to this topic**, choose **Only these AWS users**, and then type one of the following ARNs, depending on your region:

        * for Asia Pacific (Mumbai) - *arn:aws:iam::162588757376:root*
        * for Asia Pacific (Seoul) - *arn:aws:iam::526946625049:root*
        * for Asia Pacific (Sydney) - *arn:aws:iam::454640832652:root*
        * for Asia Pacific (Tokyo) - *arn:aws:iam::406045910587:root*
        * for EU (Frankfurt) - *arn:aws:iam::537503971621:root*
        * for EU (Ireland) - *arn:aws:iam::357557129151:root*
        * for US East (Northern Virginia) - *arn:aws:iam::316112463485:root*
        * for US East (Ohio) - *arn:aws:iam::646659390643:root*
        * for US West (Northern California) - *arn:aws:iam::166987590008:root*
        * for US West (Oregon) - *arn:aws:iam::758058086616:root*
        * for AWS GovCloud (US) - *arn:aws-us-gov:iam:: 850862329162:root*

Amazon Inspector Findings

Findings are potential security issues discovered during the Amazon Inspector's assessment of the selected assessment target. Findings are displayed in the Amazon Inspector console or via the API, and contain both a detailed description of the security issues and recommendations for resolving them.

Once Amazon Inspector generates the findings, you can track them by assigning Amazon Inspector-specific attributes to them. These attributes consist of key-value pairs.

Tracking findings with attributes can be quite useful for driving the work flow of your security strategy. For example, once you create and run an assessment, it generates a list of findings of various severity, urgency, and interest to you, based on your security goals and approach. You might want to follow one finding's recommendation steps right away to resolve a potentially urgent security issue, or you might want to postpone resolving another finding until your next upcoming service update. For example, to track a finding to resolve right away, you can create and assign to a finding an attribute with a key-value pair of **Status / Urgent**. You could also use attributes to distribute the workload of resolving potential security issues. For example, to give Bob (who is a security engineer on your team) the task of resolving a finding, you can assign to a finding an attribute with a key-value pair of **Assigned Engineer / Bob**.

Working with Findings

Complete the following procedure on any of the generated Amazon Inspector findings:

To locate, analyze, and assign attributes to findings

1. Sign in to the AWS Management Console and open the Amazon Inspector console at https://console.aws. amazon.com/inspector/.

2. After you run an assessment, navigate to the **Findings** page in the Amazon Inspector console to view your findings.

   You can also see your findings in the **Notable Findings** section on the **Dashboard** page of the Amazon Inspector console. **Note**
   You cannot view the findings generated by an assessment run while it is still in progress. However, you can view a subset of findings if you stop the assessment before it completes its duration. In a production environment, we recommend that you let every assessment run through its entire duration so that it can produce a full set of findings.

3. To view the details of a specific finding, choose the **Expand** widget next to that finding. The details of the finding include the following:

   - Name of the assessment target that includes the EC2 instance where this finding was registered
   - Name of the assessment template that was used to produce this finding
   - Assessment run start time
   - Assessment run end time
   - Assessment run status
   - Name of the rules package that includes the rule that triggered this finding
   - Name of the finding
   - Severity of the finding
   - Native severity details from Common Vulnerability Scoring System (CVSS), including CVSS vector and CVSS score metrics (including CVSS version 2.0 and 3.0) for the findings triggered by the rules in the Common Vulnerabilities and Exposures rules package. For more details about the CVSS, see https://www.first.org/cvss/.
   - Native severity details from the Center of Internet Security (CIS), including the CIS weight metric for the findings triggered by the rules in the CIS Benchmarks package. For more information about CIS weight metric, see https://www.cisecurity.org/.
   - Description of the finding

- Recommended steps that you can complete to fix the potential security issue described by the finding

4. To assign attributes to a finding, choose a finding, and then choose **Add/Edit Attributes**.

   You can also assign attributes to findings as you create a new assessment template by configuring the new template to automatically assign attributes to all findings generated by the assessment run. To do this, you can use the **Key** and **Value** fields from the **Tags for findings from this assessment** field. For more information, see Amazon Inspector Assessment Templates and Assessment Runs.

5. To export findings to a spreadsheet, click the down arrow button located in the upper right corner of the **Amazon Inspector - Findings** page. Then, in the pop up window, choose to **Export all columns** or to **Export visible columns**.

6. To show or hide columns for the generated findings and to filter through the generated findings, click the settings wheel icon located in the upper right corner of the **Amazon Inspector - Findings** page.

7. To delete findings, navigate to the **Assessment runs** page and select the run that resulted in the findings that you want to delete. Then choose **Delete**. When prompted for confirmation, click **Yes. Important** You cannot delete individual findings in Amazon Inspector. When you delete an assessment run, all findings and all versions of the report from that run are also deleted.

   You can also delete an assessment run by using the DeleteAssessmentRun API.

Assessment Reports

An assessment report is a document that details what is tested in the assessment run, and the results of the assessment. The results of your assessment are formatted into standard reports, which can be generated to share results within your team for remediation actions, to enrich compliance audit data, or to store for future reference. An Amazon Inspector assessment report can be generated for an assessment run once it has been successfully completed.

Note

You can only generate reports for assessment runs that took place or will take place after 4/25/2017, which is when assessment reports in Amazon Inspector became available.

You can view the following types of assessment reports:

- **Findings report** - this report contains the following information:
  - Executive summary of the assessment
  - EC2 instances evaluated during the assessment run
  - Rules packages included in the assessment run
  - Detailed information about each finding, including all EC2 instances that had the finding
- **Full report** - this report contains all the information that is included in a findings report, and additionally provides the list of rules that passed on all instances in the assessment target.

To generate an assessment report

1. On the **Assessment runs** page, locate the assessment run for which you want to generate a report and make sure that its status is set to **Analysis complete**.

2. Choose the reports icon under the **Reports** column for this assessment run. **Important**
   The reports icon is present in the **Reports** column only for those assessment runs that took place or will take place after 4/25/2017, which is when assessment reports in Amazon Inspector became available.

3. In the **Assessment report** pop up window, select the type of report you want to view (you can choose between a **Findings** or a **Full** report) and the report format (HTML or PDF), and then choose **Generate report**.

You can also generate assessment reports via the GetAssessmentReport API.

To delete an assessment report, perform the following procedure:

To delete an assessment report

- In the **Assessment runs** page, choose the run that the report that you want to delete is based on, and then choose **Delete**. When prompted for confirmation, choose **Yes**. **Important**
  In Amazon Inspector, you cannot delete individual reports. When you delete an assessment run, all versions of the report from that run and all findings are also deleted.

  You can also delete an assessment run by using the DeleteAssessmentRun API.

Amazon Inspector Rules Packages and Rules

You can use Amazon Inspector to assess your assessment targets (collections of AWS resources) for potential security issues and vulnerabilities. Amazon Inspector compares the behavior and the security configuration of the assessment targets to selected security *rules packages*. In the context of Amazon Inspector, a *rule* is a security check that Amazon Inspector performs during the assessment run.

In Amazon Inspector, rules are grouped together into distinct *rules packages* either by category, severity, or pricing. This gives you choices for the kinds of analysis that you can perform. For example, Amazon Inspector offers a large number of rules that you can use to assess your applications. But you might want to include a smaller subset of the available rules to target a specific area of concern or to uncover specific security problems. Companies with large IT departments might want to determine whether their application is exposed to any security threat, while others might want to concentrate only on issues with the severity level of **High**.

- Severity Levels for Rules in Amazon Inspector
- Rules Packages in Amazon Inspector

Severity Levels for Rules in Amazon Inspector

Each Amazon Inspector rule has an assigned severity level. This reduces the need to prioritize one rule over another in your analyses. It can also help you determine your response when a rule highlights a potential problem. **High**, **Medium**, and **Low** levels all indicate a security issue that can result in compromised information confidentiality, integrity, and availability within your assessment target. The **Informational** level simply highlights a security configuration detail of your assessment target. Following are recommended ways to respond to each:

- **High** – Describes a security issue that can result in a compromise of the information confidentiality, integrity, and availability within your assessment target. We recommend that you treat this security issue as an emergency and implement an immediate remediation.
- **Medium** – Describes a security issue that can result in a compromise of the information confidentiality, integrity, and availability within your assessment target. We recommend that you fix this issue at the next possible opportunity, for example, during your next service update.
- **Low** - Describes a security issue that can result in a compromise of the information confidentiality, integrity, and availability within your assessment target. We recommend that you fix this issue as part of one of your future service updates.
- **Informational** – Describes a particular security configuration detail of your assessment target. Based on your business and organization goals, you can either simply make note of this information or use it to improve the security of your assessment target.

Rules Packages in Amazon Inspector

The following are the rules packages available in Amazon Inspector:

- Common Vulnerabilities and Exposures
- Center for Internet Security (CIS) Benchmarks
- Security Best Practices
- Runtime Behavior Analysis

Common Vulnerabilities and Exposures

The rules in this package help verify whether the EC2 instances in your assessment targets are exposed to common vulnerabilities and exposures (CVEs). Attacks can exploit unpatched vulnerabilities to compromise the confidentiality, integrity, or availability of your service or data. The CVE system provides a reference method for publicly known information security vulnerabilities and exposures. For more information, go to https://cve.mitre.org/.

If a particular CVE appears in a *finding* produced by an Amazon Inspector assessment, you can search https://cve.mitre.org/ for the CVE's ID (for example, **CVE-2009-0021**). The search results can provide detailed information about this CVE, its severity, and how to mitigate it.

The rules included in this package help you assess whether your EC2 instances are exposed to the CVEs in the following list: https://s3-us-west-2.amazonaws.com/rules-engine/CVEList.txt. The CVE rules package is updated regularly; this list includes the CVEs that are included in assessments runs that occur at the same time that this list is retrieved.

For more information, see Rules Packages Availability Across Supported Operating Systems.

Center for Internet Security (CIS) Benchmarks

The CIS Security Benchmarks program provides well-defined, un-biased and consensus-based industry best practices to help organizations assess and improve their security. Amazon Web Services is a CIS Security Benchmarks Member company and the list of Amazon Inspector certifications can be viewed here.

Amazon Inspector currently provides the following CIS Certified rules packages to help establish secure configuration postures for the following operating systems:

- Amazon Linux 2015.03 (CIS Benchmark for Amazon Linux 2014.09-2015.03, v1.1.0, Level 1 Profile)
- Windows Server 2008 R2 (CIS Benchmark for Microsoft Windows 2008 R2, v3.0.0, Level 1 Domain Controller)
- Windows Server 2008 R2 (CIS Benchmark for Microsoft Windows 2008 R2, v3.0.0, Level 1 Member Server Profile)
- Windows Server 2012 R2 (CIS Benchmark for Microsoft Windows Server 2012 R2, v2.2.0, Level 1 Member Server Profile)
- Windows Server 2012 R2 (CIS Benchmark for Microsoft Windows Server 2012 R2, v2.2.0, Level 1 Domain Controller Profile)
- Windows Server 2012 (CIS Benchmark for Microsoft Windows Server 2012 non-R2, v2.0.0, Level 1 Member Server Profile)
- Windows Server 2012 (CIS Benchmark for Microsoft Windows Server 2012 non-R2, v2.0.0, Level 1 Domain Controller Profile)

If a particular CIS benchmark appears in a finding produced by an Amazon Inspector assessment run, you can download a detailed PDF description of the benchmark from https://benchmarks.cisecurity.org/ (free registration required). The benchmark document provides detailed information about this CIS benchmark, its severity, and how to mitigate it.

For more information, see Rules Packages Availability Across Supported Operating Systems.

Security Best Practices

The rules in this package help determine whether your systems are configured securely.

Important

In this release of Amazon Inspector, you can include in your assessment targets EC2 instances that are running either Linux-based or Windows-based operating systems.

During an assessment run, the rules in all the packages described in this topic generate findings **only** for the EC2 instances that are running Linux-based operating systems. The rules in these packages do NOT generate findings for EC2 instances that are running Windows-based operating systems.

For more information, see Rules Packages Availability Across Supported Operating Systems.

Topics

- Disable Root Login over SSH
- Support SSH Version 2 Only
- Disable Password Authentication Over SSH
- Configure Password Maximum Age
- Configure Password Minimum Length
- Configure Password Complexity
- Enable ASLR
- Enable DEP
- Configure Permissions for System Directories

Disable Root Login over SSH

This rule helps determine whether the SSH daemon is configured to permit logging in to your EC2 instance as root .

Severity: Medium

Finding

There is an instance in your assessment target that is configured to allow users to log in with root credentials over SSH. This increases the likelihood of a successful brute-force attack.

Resolution

We recommend that you configure your EC2 instance to prevent root account logins over SSH. Instead, log in as a non-root user and use **sudo** to escalate privileges when necessary. To disable SSH root account logins, set **PermitRootLogin** to **no** in **/etc/ssh/sshd_config** and restart sshd.

Support SSH Version 2 Only

This rule helps determine whether your EC2 instances are configured to support SSH protocol version 1.

Severity: Medium

Finding

An EC2 instance in your assessment target is configured to support SSH 1, which contains inherent design flaws that greatly reduce its security.

Resolution

We recommend that you configure EC2 instances in your assessment target to support only SSH 2 and higher. For OpenSSH, you can achieve this by setting **Protocol 2** in **/etc/ssh/sshd_config**. For more information, see** man sshd_config**.

Disable Password Authentication Over SSH

This rule helps determine whether your EC2 instances are configured to support password authentication over the SSH protocol.

Severity: Medium

Finding

An EC2 instance in your assessment target is configured to support password authentication over SSH. Password authentication is susceptible to brute-force attacks and should be disabled in favor of key-based authentication where possible.

Resolution

We recommend that you disable password authentication over SSH on your EC2 instances and enable support for key-based authentication instead. This significantly reduces the likelihood of a successful brute-force attack. For more information, see https://aws.amazon.com/articles/1233/. If password authentication is supported, it is important to restrict access to the SSH server to trusted IP addresses.

Configure Password Maximum Age

This rule helps determine whether the maximum age for passwords is configured on your EC2 instances.

Severity - Medium

Finding

An EC2 instance in your assessment target is not configured for a maximum age for passwords.

Resolution

If you are using passwords, we recommend that you configure a maximum age for passwords on all EC2 instances in your assessment target. This requires users to regularly change their passwords and reduces the chances of a successful password guessing attack. To fix this issue for existing users, use the **chage** command. To configure a maximum age for passwords for all future users, edit the **PASS_MAX_DAYS** field in the **/etc/login.defs** file.

Configure Password Minimum Length

This rule helps determine whether a minimum length for passwords is configured on your EC2 instances.

Severity: Medium

Finding

An EC2 instance in your assessment target is not configured for a minimum length for passwords.

Resolution

If you are using passwords, we recommend that you configure a minimum length for passwords on all EC2 instances in your assessment target. Enforcing a minimum password length reduces the risk of a successful password guessing attack. To enforce minimum password lengths, set the **minlen** parameter of **pam_cracklib.so** in your PAM configuration. For more information, see **man pam_cracklib**.

Configure Password Complexity

This rule helps determine whether a password complexity mechanism is configured on your EC2 instances.

Severity: Medium

Finding

No password complexity mechanism or restrictions are configured on EC2 instances in your assessment target. This allows users to set simple passwords, thereby increasing the chances of unauthorized users gaining access and misusing accounts.

Resolution

If you are using passwords, we recommend that you configure all EC2 instances in your assessment target to require a level of password complexity. You can do this by using pwquality.conf "lcredit", "ucredit", "dcredit", and "ocredit" settings. For more information, see https://linux.die.net/man/5/pwquality.conf . If pwquality.conf is not available on your instance, you can set the "lcredit", "ucredit", "dcredit", and "ocredit" settings using **pam_cracklib.so**. For more information, see **man pam_cracklib**.

Enable ASLR

This rule helps determine whether address space layout randomization (ASLR) is enabled on the operating systems of the EC2 instances in your assessment target.

Severity: Medium

Finding

An EC2 instance in your assessment target does not have ASLR enabled.

Resolution

To improve the security of your assessment target, we recommend that you enable ASLR on the operating systems of all EC2 instances in your assessment target by running echo 2 | sudo tee /proc/sys/kernel/randomize_va_space.

Enable DEP

This rule helps determine whether Data Execution Prevention (DEP) is enabled on the operating systems of the EC2 instances in your assessment target.

Severity: Medium

Finding

An EC2 instance in your assessment target does not have DEP enabled.

Resolution

We recommend that you enable DEP on the operating systems of all EC2 instances in your assessment target. Enabling DEP protects your instances from security compromises using buffer-overflow techniques.

Configure Permissions for System Directories

This rule checks permissions on system directories that contain binaries and system configuration information to make sure that only the root user (a user who logs in by using root account credentials) has write permissions for these directories.

Severity: High

Finding

An EC2 instance in your assessment target contains a system directory that is writable by non-root users.

Resolution

To improve the security of your assessment target and to prevent privilege escalation by malicious local users, configure all system directories on all EC2 instances in your assessment target to be writable only by users who log in by using root account credentials.

Runtime Behavior Analysis

These rules analyze the behavior of your instances during an assessment run, and provide guidance about how to make your EC2 instances more secure.

For more information, see Rules Packages Availability Across Supported Operating Systems.

Topics

- Insecure Client Protocols (Login)
- Insecure Client Protocols (General)
- Unused Listening TCP Ports
- Insecure Server Protocols
- Software Without DEP
- Root Process with Insecure Permissions

Insecure Client Protocols (Login)

This rule detects a client's use of insecure protocols to log in to remote machines.

Important
In this release of Amazon Inspector, you can include in your assessment targets EC2 instances that are running either Linux-based or Windows-based operating systems.
This rule generates findings for the EC2 instances that are running either Linux-based or Windows-based operating systems.

Severity: Medium

Finding

An EC2 instance in your assessment target uses insecure protocols to connect to a remote host for login. These protocols pass credentials in the clear, increasing the risk of credential theft.

Resolution

It is recommended that you replace these insecure protocols with secure protocols, such as SSH.

Insecure Client Protocols (General)

This rule detects a client's use of insecure protocols

Important
In this release of Amazon Inspector, you can include in your assessment targets EC2 instances that are running either Linux-based or Windows-based operating systems.
This rule generates findings for the EC2 instances that are running either Linux-based or Windows-based operating systems.

Severity: Low

Finding

An EC2 instance in your assessment target uses insecure protocols to connect to a remote host. These protocols pass traffic in the clear, increasing the risk of a successful traffic interception attack.

Resolution

It is recommended that you replace these insecure protocols with encrypted versions.

Unused Listening TCP Ports

This rule detects listening TCP ports that may not be required by the assessment target.

Important
In this release of Amazon Inspector, you can include in your assessment targets EC2 instances that are running either Linux-based or Windows-based operating systems.
This rule generates findings for the EC2 instances that are running either Linux-based or Windows-based operating systems.

Severity: Informational

Finding

An EC2 instance in your assessment target is listening on TCP ports but no traffic to these ports was seen during the assessment run.

Resolution

To reduce the attack surface area of your deployments, we recommend that you disable network services that you do not use. Where network services are required, we recommend that you employ network control mechanisms such as VPC ACLs, EC2 security groups, and firewalls to limit exposure of that service.

Insecure Server Protocols

This rule helps determine whether your EC2 instances allow support for insecure and unencrypted ports/services such as FTP, Telnet, HTTP, IMAP, POP version 3, SMTP, SNMP versions 1 and 2, rsh, and rlogin.

Important
In this release of Amazon Inspector, you can include in your assessment targets EC2 instances that are running either Linux-based or Windows-based operating systems.
This rule generates findings for the EC2 instances that are running either Linux-based or Windows-based operating systems.

Severity: Informational

Finding

An EC2 instance in your assessment target is configured to support insecure protocols.

Resolution

We recommend that you disable insecure protocols that are supported on an EC2 instance in your assessment target and replace them with secure alternatives as listed below:

- Disable Telnet, rsh, and rlogin and replace them with SSH. Where this is not possible, you should ensure that the insecure service is protected by appropriate network access controls such as VPC network ACLs and EC2 security groups.

- Replace FTP with SCP or SFTP where possible. Where this is not possible, you should ensure that the FTP server is protected by appropriate network access controls such as VPC network ACLs and EC2 security groups.
- Replace HTTP with HTTPS where possible. For more information specific to the web server in question, see http://nginx/.org/en/docs/http/configuring/_https/_servers/.html and http://httpd/.apache/.org/docs/2/.4/ssl/ssl/_howto/.html/.
- Disable IMAP, POP3, and SMTP services if not required. If required, we recommend that these email protocols are used with encrypted protocols such as TLS.
- Disable SNMP service if not required. If required, replace SNMP v1and v2 with the more secure SNMP v3, which uses encrypted communication.

Software Without DEP

This rule detects the presence of third-party software that is compiled without support for Data Execution Prevention (DEP). DEP increases system security by defending against stack-based buffer overflow and other memory corruption attacks.

Important
In this release of Amazon Inspector, you can include in your assessment targets EC2 instances that are running either Linux-based or Windows-based operating systems.
During an assessment run, this rule generates findings **only** for the EC2 instances that are running Linux-based operating systems. This rule does NOT generate findings for EC2 instances that are running Windows-based operating systems.

Severity: Medium

Finding

There are executable files on an EC2 instance in your assessment target that do not support DEP.

Resolution

It is recommended that you uninstall this software from your assessment target if you are not using it, or contact the vendor to get an updated version of this software with DEP enabled.

Root Process with Insecure Permissions

This rule helps detect root processes that load modules that can be modified by unauthorized users.

Important
In this release of Amazon Inspector, you can include in your assessment targets EC2 instances that are running either Linux-based or Windows-based operating systems.
During an assessment run, this rule generates findings **only** for the EC2 instances that are running Linux-based operating systems. This rule does NOT generate findings for EC2 instances that are running Windows-based operating systems.

Severity: High

Finding

There is an instance in your assessment target with one or more root-owned processes that make use of shared objects that are vulnerable to unauthorized modification. These shared objects have inappropriate permissions/ownership and are therefore vulnerable to tampering.

Resolution

To improve the security of your assessment target, it is recommended that you correct the permissions on the relevant modules to ensure that they are writable only by root.

Rules Packages Availability Across Supported Operating Systems

The following table describes Amazon Inspector rules packages' availability across supported operating systems that you can run on the EC2 instances included in your assessment targets.

Note
For more information about supported operating systems, see Amazon Inspector Supported Operating Systems and Regions.

Supported Operating Systems	Common Vulnerabilities and Exposures	CIS Benchmarks	Security Best Practices	Runtime Behavior Analysis
Amazon Linux 2 2017.12	Supported		Supported	Supported
Amazon Linux 2018.03	Supported		Supported	Supported
Amazon Linux 2017.09	Supported		Supported	Supported
Amazon Linux 2017.03	Supported		Supported	Supported
Amazon Linux 2016.09	Supported		Supported	Supported
Amazon Linux 2016.03	Supported		Supported	Supported
Amazon Linux 2015.09	Supported		Supported	Supported
Amazon Linux 2015.03	Supported	Supported	Supported	Supported
Amazon Linux 2014.09	Supported		Supported	
Amazon Linux 2014.03	Supported		Supported	
Amazon Linux 2013.09	Supported		Supported	
Amazon Linux 2013.03	Supported		Supported	
Amazon Linux 2012.09	Supported		Supported	
Amazon Linux 2012.03	Supported		Supported	
Ubuntu 18.04 LTS	Supported		Supported	Supported
Ubuntu 16.04 LTS	Supported		Supported	Supported
Ubuntu 14.04 LTS	Supported		Supported	Supported
Debian 9.0 - 9.4	Supported		Supported	
RHEL 6.2 - 6.9 and 7.2 - 7.5	Supported		Supported	Supported
CentOS 6.2 - 6.9 and 7.2 - 7.5	Supported		Supported	Supported
Windows Server 2012 R2	Supported	Supported		Supported
Windows Server 2012	Supported	Supported		Supported
Windows Server 2008 R2	Supported	Supported		Supported

Supported Operating Systems	Common Vulnerabilities and Exposures	CIS Benchmarks	Security Best Practices	Runtime Behavior Analysis
Windows Server 2016 Base	Supported			Supported

Logging Amazon Inspector API Calls with AWS CloudTrail

Amazon Inspector is integrated with CloudTrail, a service that captures all the Amazon InspectorAPI calls and delivers the log files to an Amazon S3 bucket that you specify. CloudTrail captures API calls from the Amazon Inspector console or from your code to the Amazon Inspector APIs. Using the information collected by CloudTrail, you can determine the request that was made to Amazon Inspector, the source IP address from which the request was made, who made the request, when it was made, and so on.

To learn more about CloudTrail, including how to configure and enable it, see the AWS CloudTrail User Guide.

Amazon Inspector Information in CloudTrail

When CloudTrail logging is enabled in your AWS account, API calls made to Amazon Inspector actions are tracked in CloudTrail log files, where they are written with other AWS service records. CloudTrail determines when to create and write to a new file based on a time period and file size.

All Amazon Inspector actions are logged by CloudTrail and are documented in the Amazon Inspector API Reference.

For example, calls to the **CreateAssessmentTarget**, **CreateAssessmentTemplate** and **StartAssessmentRun** sections generate entries in the CloudTrail log files.

Note
For the Amazon Inspector integration with CloudTrail, for the List* and Describe* APIs, for example, ListAssessmentTargets or `DescribeAssessmentTargets`, only the request information is logged; for the Create*, Start*, Stop*, and all other APIs, for example, `CreateResourceGroup`, both the request and response information is logged.

Every log entry contains information about who generated the request. The user identity information in the log entry helps you determine the following:

- Whether the request was made with root or IAM user credentials
- Whether the request was made with temporary security credentials for a role or federated user
- Whether the request was made by another AWS service

For more information, see the CloudTrail userIdentity Element.

You can store your log files in your Amazon S3 bucket for as long as you want, but you can also define Amazon S3 lifecycle rules to archive or delete log files automatically. By default, your log files are encrypted with Amazon S3 server-side encryption (SSE).

If you want to be notified upon log file delivery, you can configure CloudTrail to publish Amazon SNS notifications when new log files are delivered. For more information, see Configuring Amazon SNS Notifications for CloudTrail.

You can also aggregate Amazon Inspector log files from multiple AWS regions and multiple AWS accounts into a single Amazon S3 bucket.

For more information, see Receiving CloudTrail Log Files from Multiple Regions and Receiving CloudTrail Log Files from Multiple Accounts.

Understanding Amazon Inspector Log File Entries

CloudTrail log files can contain one or more log entries. Each entry lists multiple JSON-formatted events. A log entry represents a single request from any source and includes information about the requested action, the date and time of the action, request parameters, and so on. Log entries are not an ordered stack trace of the public API calls, so they do not appear in any specific order.

The following example shows a CloudTrail log entry that demonstrates the Amazon Inspector CreateResourceGroup action:

```
1   {
2   "eventVersion": "1.03",
3   "userIdentity": {
4       "type": "AssumedRole",
5       "principalId": "AIDACKCEVSQ6C2EXAMPLE",
6       "arn": "arn:aws:iam::444455556666:user/Alice",
7       "accountId": "444455556666",
8       "accessKeyId": "AKIAI44QH8DHBEXAMPLE",
9       "sessionContext": {
10          "attributes": {
11              "mfaAuthenticated": "false",
12              "creationDate": "2016-04-14T17:05:54Z"
13          },
14          "sessionIssuer": {
15              "type": "Role",
16              "principalId": "AIDACKCEVSQ6C2EXAMPLE",
17              "arn": "arn:aws:iam::444455556666:user/Alice",
18              "accountId": "444455556666",
19              "userName": "Alice"
20          }
21      }
22  },
23  "eventTime": "2016-04-14T17:12:34Z",
24  "eventSource": "inspector.amazonaws.com",
25  "eventName": "CreateResourceGroup",
26  "awsRegion": "us-west-2",
27  "sourceIPAddress": "205.251.233.179",
28  "userAgent": "console.amazonaws.com",
29  "requestParameters": {
30      "resourceGroupTags": [
31          {
32              "key": "Name",
33              "value": "ExampleEC2Instance"
34          }
35      ]
36  },
37  "responseElements": {
38      "resourceGroupArn": "arn:aws:inspector:us-west-2:444455556666:resourcegroup/0-oclRMp8B"
39  },
40  "requestID": "148256d2-0264-11e6-a9b5-b98a7d3b840f",
41  "eventID": "e5ea533e-eede-46cc-94f6-0d08e6306ff0",
42  "eventType": "AwsApiCall",
43  "apiVersion": "v20160216",
44  "recipientAccountId": "444455556666"
45  }
```

From this event information, you can determine that the request was made to create a new resource group (using the Amazon Inspector CreateResourceGroup API) with the tag key-value pair of Name and ExampleEC2Instance to identify the EC2 instance to be included in the new resource group. You can also see that the request was made by an IAM user named Alice on April 14, 2016.

The following example shows a CloudTrail log entry that demonstrates the Amazon Inspector DescribeAssessmentTargets action:

```
1    {
2    "eventVersion": "1.03",
3    "userIdentity": {
4        "type": "AssumedRole",
5        "principalId": "AIDACKCEVSQ6C2EXAMPLE",
6        "arn": "arn:aws:iam::444455556666:user/Alice",
7        "accountId": "444455556666",
8        "accessKeyId": "AKIAI44QH8DHBEXAMPLE",
9        "sessionContext": {
10            "attributes": {
11                "mfaAuthenticated": "false",
12                "creationDate": "2016-04-14T17:05:54Z"
13            },
14            "sessionIssuer": {
15                "type": "Role",
16                "principalId": "AIDACKCEVSQ6C2EXAMPLE",
17                "arn": "arn:aws:iam::444455556666:user/Alice",
18                "accountId": "444455556666",
19                "userName": "Alice"
20            }
21        }
22    },
23        "eventTime": "2016-04-14T17:30:49Z",
24        "eventSource": "inspector.amazonaws.com",
25        "eventName": "DescribeAssessmentTargets",
26        "awsRegion": "us-west-2",
27        "sourceIPAddress": "205.251.233.179",
28        "userAgent": "console.amazonaws.com",
29        "requestParameters": {
30          "assessmentTargetArns": [
31            "arn:aws:inspector:us-west-2:444455556666:target/0-ABcQzlXc",
32            "arn:aws:inspector:us-west-2:444455556666:target/0-nvgVhaxX"
33          ]
34        },
35        "responseElements": null,
36        "requestID": "a103f654-0266-11e6-93e6-890abdd45f56",
37        "eventID": "bd7de684-2b2f-4d45-8cef-d22bf17bcb13",
38        "eventType": "AwsApiCall",
39        "apiVersion": "v20160216",
40        "recipientAccountId": "444455556666"
41    },
```

From this event information, you can determine that the request was made to describe two assessment targets with corresponding ARNs of arn:aws:inspector:us-west-2:444455556666:target/0-ABcQzlXc and arn:aws:inspector:us-west-2:444455556666:target/0-nvgVhaxX (using the Amazon Inspector `DescribeAssessmentTargets` API). You can also see that the request was made by an IAM user named `Alice` on April 14, 2016. Note that per the Amazon Inspector implementation of the integration with CloudTrail, because this is a List* API, only the request information is logged (the ARNs to specify the assessment targets to be described). The list of response elements is not logged and left null.

Monitoring Amazon Inspector Using CloudWatch

You can monitor Amazon Inspector using Amazon CloudWatch, which collects and processes raw data into readable, near real-time metrics. These statistics are recorded in CloudWatch so that you can access historical information and gain a better perspective on how Amazon Inspector is performing.

By default, Amazon Inspector sends metric data to CloudWatch in 5-minute periods. You can use the AWS Management Console, the AWS CLI, or an API to list the metrics that Amazon Inspector sends to CloudWatch.

For more information about Amazon CloudWatch, see the Amazon CloudWatch User Guide.

Amazon Inspector CloudWatch Metrics

The Amazon Inspector namespace includes the following metrics:

AssessmentTargetARN metrics:

Metric	Description
TotalMatchingAgents	Number of agents matching this target
TotalHealthyAgents	Number of agents matching this target that are healthy
TotalAssessmentRuns	Number of assessment runs for this target
TotalAssessmentRunFindings	Number of findings for this target

AssessmentTemplateARN metrics:

Metric	Description
TotalMatchingAgents	Number of agents matching this template
TotalHealthyAgents	Number of agents matching this template that are healthy
TotalAssessmentRuns	Number of assessment runs for this template
TotalAssessmentRunFindings	Number of findings for this template

Aggregate metrics

Metric	Description
TotalAssessmentRuns	Number of assessment runs in this AWS account

Configuring Amazon Inspector Using AWS CloudFormation

The following topics contains reference information for all Amazon Inspector resources that are supported by AWS CloudFormation:

- AWS::Inspector::AssessmentTarget
- AWS::Inspector::AssessmentTemplate
- AWS::Inspector::ResourceGroup

Important
For reference information on all Amazon Inspector rules packages' ARNs in all supported regions, see Appendix - Amazon Inspector Rules Packages' ARNs.

Authentication and Access Control for Amazon Inspector

Access to Amazon Inspector requires credentials that AWS can use to authenticate your requests. Those credentials must have permissions to access AWS resources, such as Amazon Inspector assessment targets, assessment templates, or findings. The following sections provide details on how you can use AWS Identity and Access Management (IAM) and Amazon Inspector to help secure your resources by controlling who can access them:

- Authentication
- Access Control

Authentication

You can access AWS as any of the following types of identities:

- **AWS account root user** – When you first create an AWS account, you begin with a single sign-in identity that has complete access to all AWS services and resources in the account. This identity is called the AWS account *root user* and is accessed by signing in with the email address and password that you used to create the account. We strongly recommend that you do not use the root user for your everyday tasks, even the administrative ones. Instead, adhere to the best practice of using the root user only to create your first IAM user. Then securely lock away the root user credentials and use them to perform only a few account and service management tasks.

- **IAM user** – An IAM user is an identity within your AWS account that has specific custom permissions (for example, permissions to create a directory in AWS Directory Service). You can use an IAM user name and password to sign in to secure AWS webpages like the AWS Management Console, AWS Discussion Forums, or the AWS Support Center.

  In addition to a user name and password, you can also generate access keys for each user. You can use these keys when you access AWS services programmatically, either through one of the several SDKs or by using the AWS Command Line Interface (CLI). The SDK and CLI tools use the access keys to cryptographically sign your request. If you don't use AWS tools, you must sign the request yourself. AWS Directory Service supports *Signature Version 4*, a protocol for authenticating inbound API requests. For more information about authenticating requests, see Signature Version 4 Signing Process in the *AWS General Reference*.

- **IAM role** – An IAM role is an IAM identity that you can create in your account that has specific permissions. It is similar to an *IAM user*, but it is not associated with a specific person. An IAM role enables you to obtain temporary access keys that can be used to access AWS services and resources. IAM roles with temporary credentials are useful in the following situations:

  - **Federated user access** – Instead of creating an IAM user, you can use existing user identities from AWS Directory Service, your enterprise user directory, or a web identity provider. These are known as *federated users*. AWS assigns a role to a federated user when access is requested through an identity provider. For more information about federated users, see Federated Users and Roles in the *IAM User Guide*.

  - **AWS service access** – You can use an IAM role in your account to grant an AWS service permissions to access your account's resources. For example, you can create a role that allows Amazon Redshift to access an Amazon S3 bucket on your behalf and then load data from that bucket into an Amazon

Redshift cluster. For more information, see Creating a Role to Delegate Permissions to an AWS Service in the *IAM User Guide*.

- **Applications running on Amazon EC2** – You can use an IAM role to manage temporary credentials for applications that are running on an EC2 instance and making AWS API requests. This is preferable to storing access keys within the EC2 instance. To assign an AWS role to an EC2 instance and make it available to all of its applications, you create an instance profile that is attached to the instance. An instance profile contains the role and enables programs that are running on the EC2 instance to get temporary credentials. For more information, see Using an IAM Role to Grant Permissions to Applications Running on Amazon EC2 Instances in the *IAM User Guide*.

Access Control

You can have valid credentials to authenticate your requests, but unless you have permissions you cannot create or access Amazon Inspector resources. For example, you must have permissions to create an Amazon Inspector assessment target and an assessment template to start an assessment run.

The following sections describe how to manage permissions for Amazon Inspector. We recommend that you read the overview first.

- Overview of Managing Access Permissions to Your Amazon Inspector Resources
- Using Identity-based Policies (IAM Policies) for Amazon Inspector
- Amazon Inspector API Permissions: Actions, Resources, and Conditions Reference

Overview of Managing Access Permissions to Your Amazon Inspector Resources

Every AWS resource is owned by an AWS account, and permissions to create or access a resource are governed by permissions policies. An account administrator can attach permissions policies to IAM identities (that is, users, groups, and roles), and some services (such as AWS Lambda) also support attaching permissions policies to resources.

Note
An *account administrator* (or administrator user) is a user with administrator privileges. For more information, see IAM Best Practices in the *IAM User Guide*.

When granting permissions, you decide who is getting the permissions, the resources they get permissions for, and the specific actions that you want to allow on those resources.

Topics

- Amazon Inspector Resources and Operations
- Understanding Resource Ownership
- Managing Access to Resources
- Specifying Policy Elements: Actions, Effects, Resources, and Principals
- Specifying Conditions in a Policy

Amazon Inspector Resources and Operations

In Amazon Inspector, the primary resources are resource groups, assessment targets, assessment templates, assessment runs, and findings. These resources have unique Amazon Resource Names (ARNs) associated with them as shown in the following table.

Resource Type	ARN Format
Resource group	arn:aws:inspector:*region*:*account-id*:resourcegroup/*ID*
Assessment target	arn:aws:inspector:*region*:*account-id*:target/*ID*
Assessment template	arn:aws:inspector:*region*:*account-id*:target/*ID*:template:*ID*
Assessment run	arn:aws:inspector:*region*:*account-id*:target/*ID*/template/*ID*/run/*ID*
Finding	arn:aws:inspector:*region*:*account-id*:target/*ID*/template/*ID*/run/*ID*/finding/*ID*

Amazon Inspector provides a set of operations to work with the Amazon Inspector resources. For a list of available operations, see Actions.

Understanding Resource Ownership

A *resource owner* is the AWS account that created the resource. That is, the resource owner is the AWS account of the *principal entity* (the root account, an IAM user, or an IAM role) that authenticates the request that creates the resource. The following examples illustrate how this works:

- If you use the root account credentials of your AWS account to create an Amazon Inspector assessment target, your AWS account is the owner of this resource.

70

- If you create an IAM user in your AWS account and grant permissions to create an Amazon Inspector assessment target to that user, the user can create an Amazon Inspector assessment target. However, your AWS account, to which the user belongs, owns the Amazon Inspector assessment target resource.
- If you create an IAM role in your AWS account with permissions to create an Amazon Inspector assessment target, anyone who can assume the role can create an Amazon Inspector assessment target. Your AWS account, to which the role belongs, owns the Amazon Inspector assessment target resource.

Managing Access to Resources

A *permissions policy* describes who has access to what. The following section explains the available options for creating permissions policies.

Note
This section discusses using IAM in the context of Amazon Inspector. It doesn't provide detailed information about the IAM service. For complete IAM documentation, see What Is IAM? in the *IAM User Guide*. For information about IAM policy syntax and descriptions, see AWS IAM Policy Reference in the *IAM User Guide*.

Policies attached to an IAM identity are referred to as *identity-based* policies (IAM policies). Policies attached to a resource are referred to as *resource-based* policies. Amazon Inspector supports only identity-based policies.

Topics

- Identity-Based Policies (IAM Policies)
- id="access-control-manage-access-resource-based.title">Resource-Based Policies

Identity-Based Policies (IAM Policies)

You can attach policies to IAM identities. For example, you can do the following:

- **Attach a permissions policy to a user or a group in your account** – An account administrator can use a permissions policy that is associated with a particular user to grant permissions for that user to create an Amazon Inspector assessment target.

- **Attach a permissions policy to a role (grant cross-account permissions)** – You can attach an identity-based permissions policy to an IAM role to grant cross-account permissions. For example, the administrator in Account A can create a role to grant cross-account permissions to another AWS account (for example, Account B) or an AWS service as follows:

  - Account A administrator creates an IAM role and attaches a permissions policy to the role that grants permissions on resources in Account A.
  - Account A administrator attaches a trust policy to the role identifying Account B as the principal who can assume the role.
  - Account B administrator can then delegate permissions to assume the role to any users in Account B. Doing this allows users in Account B to create or access resources in Account A. If you want to grant an AWS service permissions to assume the role, he principal in the trust policy can also be an AWS service principal.

  For more information about using IAM to delegate permissions, see Access Management in the *IAM User Guide*.

The following is an example policy that grants permissions for the `inspector:ListFindings` action on all resources.

```
1          {
2      "Version": "2012-10-17",
3      "Statement": [
4          {
5              "Effect": "Allow",
```

71

```
 6            "Action": [
 7                "inspector:ListFindings"
 8            ],
 9            "Resource": "*"
10        }
11    ]
12 }
```

For more information about using identity-based policies with Amazon Inspector, see Using Identity-based Policies (IAM Policies) for Amazon Inspector. For more information about users, groups, roles, and permissions, see Identities (Users, Groups, and Roles) in the *IAM User Guide*.

id="access-control-manage-access-resource-based.title">Resource-Based Policies

Other services, such as Amazon S3, also support resource-based permissions policies. For example, you can attach a policy to an S3 bucket to manage access permissions to that bucket. Amazon Inspector doesn't support resource-based policies.

Specifying Policy Elements: Actions, Effects, Resources, and Principals

For each Amazon Inspector resource (see Amazon Inspector Resources and Operations), the service defines a set of API operations (see Actions). To grant permissions for these API operations, Amazon Inspector defines a set of actions that you can specify in a policy. Note that performing an API operation can require permissions for more than one action. When granting permissions for specific actions, you also identify the resource on which the actions are allowed or denied.

The following are the most basic policy elements:

- **Resource** – In a policy, you use an Amazon Resource Name (ARN) to identify the resource to which the policy applies. For more information, see Amazon Inspector Resources and Operations.
- **Action** – You use action keywords to identify resource operations that you want to allow or deny. For example, the `inspector:ListFindings` permission allows the user permissions to perform the Amazon Inspector `ListFindings` operation.
- **Effect** – You specify the effect when the user requests the specific action—this can be either allow or deny. If you don't explicitly grant access to (allow) a resource, access is implicitly denied. You can also explicitly deny access to a resource, which you might do to make sure that a user cannot access it, even if a different policy grants access.
- **Principal** – In identity-based policies (IAM policies), the user that the policy is attached to is the implicit principal.

To learn more about IAM policy syntax and descriptions, see AWS IAM Policy Reference in the *IAM User Guide*.

For a table showing all of the Amazon Inspector API actions and the resources that they apply to, see Amazon Inspector API Permissions: Actions, Resources, and Conditions Reference.

Specifying Conditions in a Policy

When you grant permissions, you can use the IAM policy language to specify the conditions that need to be met for a policy to take effect. For example, you might want a policy to be applied only after a specific date. For more information about specifying conditions in a policy's language, see Condition in the *IAM User Guide*.

To express conditions, you use predefined condition keys. There are no condition keys specific to Amazon Inspector. However, there are AWS-wide condition keys that you can use as appropriate. For a complete list of AWS-wide keys, see Available Keys for Conditions in the *IAM User Guide*.

Using Identity-based Policies (IAM Policies) for Amazon Inspector

This topic provides examples of identity-based policies in which an account administrator can attach permissions policies to IAM identities (that is, users, groups, and roles).

Important
We recommend that you first review the introductory topics that explain the basic concepts and options available for you to manage access to your Amazon Inspector resources. For more information, see Overview of Managing Access Permissions to Your Amazon Inspector Resources.

The sections in this topic cover the following:

- Permissions Required to Use the Amazon Inspector Console
- AWS Managed (Predefined) Policies for Amazon Inspector
- Customer Managed Policy Examples

The following is an example of a permissions policy.

```
1  {
2      "Version": "2012-10-17",
3      "Statement": [
4          {
5              "Effect": "Allow",
6              "Action": [
7                  "inspector:ListFindings"
8              ],
9              "Resource": "*"
10         }
11     ]
12 }
```

This sample policy includes a statement that grants permission to list Amazon Inspector findings. Amazon Inspector doesn't support permissions for this particular action at the resource level. Therefore, the policy specifies a wildcard character (*) as the `Resource` value.

Permissions Required to Use the Amazon Inspector Console

To use the Amazon Inspector console, a user must have the permissions granted by the **AmazonInspectorFullAccess** or **AmazonInspectorReadOnlyAccess** policies described in AWS Managed (Predefined) Policies for Amazon Inspector. If you create an IAM policy that is more restrictive than the minimum required permissions described in either of these policies (for instance, the preceding example policy), the console won't function as intended for users with that IAM policy.

Note
A user that has the preceding example policy attached can successfully list Amazon Inspector findings by calling the `ListFindings` API operation or the`list-findings` CLI command.

AWS Managed (Predefined) Policies for Amazon Inspector

AWS addresses many common use cases by providing standalone IAM policies that are created and administered by AWS. These *managed policies* grant necessary permissions for common use cases so that you can avoid having to investigate which permissions are needed. For more information, see AWS Managed Policies in the *IAM User Guide*.

The following AWS managed policies, which you can attach to users in your account, are specific to Amazon Inspector:

- **AmazonInspectorFullAccess** – Provides full access to Amazon Inspector.
- **AmazonInspectorReadOnlyAccess** – Provides read-only access to Amazon Inspector.

You can also create custom IAM policies that allow users to access the required API actions and resources. You can attach these custom policies to the IAM users or groups that require those permissions.

Customer Managed Policy Examples

This section provides example user policies that grant permissions for various Amazon Inspector actions.

Note
All examples use the US West (Oregon) Region (`us-west-2`) and contain fictitious account IDs.

Topics

- Example 1: Allow a User to Perform Any Describe and List Actions on Any Amazon Inspector Resource
- Example 2: Allow a User to Perform Describe and List Actions Only on Amazon Inspector Findings

Example 1: Allow a User to Perform Any Describe and List Actions on Any Amazon Inspector Resource

The following permissions policy grants a user permissions to run all of the actions that begin with `Describe` and `List`. These actions show information about an Amazon Inspector resource, such as an assessment target or finding. Note that the wildcard character (*) in the `Resource` element indicates that the actions are allowed for all Amazon Inspector resources owned by the account.

```
1.  {
2.     "Version":"2012-10-17",
3.     "Statement":[
4.        {
5.           "Effect":"Allow",
6.           "Action": [
7.              "inspector:Describe*",
8.              "inspector:List*"
9.              ],
10.          "Resource":"*"
11.       }
12.    ]
13. }
```

Example 2: Allow a User to Perform Describe and List Actions Only on Amazon Inspector Findings

The following permissions policy grants a user permissions to run only `ListFindings` and `DescribeFindings` operations. These actions show information about Amazon Inspector findings. Note that the wildcard character (*) in the `Resource` element indicates that the actions are allowed for all of the Amazon Inspector resources owned by the account.

```
1.  {
2.     "Version":"2012-10-17",
3.     "Statement":[
4.        {
5.           "Effect":"Allow",
6.           "Action": [
7.                  "inspector:DescribeFindings",
```

```
8   8.                    "inspector:ListFindings"
9   9.            ],
10  10.           "Resource":"*"
11  11.       }
12  12.    ]
13  13. }
```

Amazon Inspector API Permissions: Actions, Resources, and Conditions Reference

The following table lists each Amazon Inspector API operation, the corresponding actions for which you can grant permissions to perform the action, and the AWS resource for which you can grant the permissions. Use it as a reference when setting up Access Control and writing permissions policies that you can attach to an IAM identity (identity-based policies). You specify the actions in the policy's `Action` field, and the resource value in the policy's `Resource` field.

You can use AWS-wide condition keys in your Amazon Inspector policies to express conditions. For a complete list of AWS-wide keys, see Available Keys for Conditions in the *IAM User Guide*.

Note

To specify an action, use the `inspector:` prefix followed by the API operation name (for example, `inspector: CreateResourceGroup`).

Amazon Inspector API and Required Permissions for Actions

Amazon Inspector API Operations	Required Permissions (API Actions)	Resources
AddAttributesToFindings	inspector:AddAttributesToFindings	*
CreateAssessmentTarget	inspector:CreateAssessmentTarget	*
CreateAssessmentTemplate	inspector:CreateAssessmentTemplate	*
CreateResourceGroup	inspector:CreateResourceGroup	*
DeleteAssessmentRun	inspector:DeleteAssessmentRun	*
DeleteAssessmentTarget	inspector:DeleteAssessmentTarget	*
DeleteAssessmentTemplate	inspector:DeleteAssessmentTemplate	*
DescribeAssessmentRuns	inspector:DescribeAssessmentRuns	*
DescribeAssessmentTargets	inspector:DescribeAssessmentTargets	*
DescribeAssessmentTemplates	inspector:DescribeAssessmentTemplates	*
DescribeCrossAccountAccessRole	inspector:DescribeCrossAccountAccessRole	*
DescribeFindings	inspector:DescribeFindings	*
DescribeResourceGroups	inspector:DescribeResourceGroups	*
DescribeRulesPackages	inspector:DescribeRulesPackages	*
GetAssessmentReport	inspector:GetAssessmentReport	*
GetTelemetryMetadata	inspector:GetTelemetryMetadata	*
ListAssessmentRunAgents	inspector:ListAssessmentRunAgents	*
ListAssessmentRuns	inspector:ListAssessmentRuns	*

Amazon Inspector API Operations	Required Permissions (API Actions)	Resources
ListAssessmentTargets	inspector:ListAssessmentTargets	*
ListAssessmentTemplates	inspector:ListAssessmentTemplates	*
ListEventSubscriptions	inspector:ListEventSubscriptions	*
ListFindings	inspector:ListFindings	*
ListRulesPackages	inspector:ListRulesPackages	*
ListTagsForResource	inspector:ListTagsForResource	*
PreviewAgents	inspector:PreviewAgents	*
RegisterCrossAccountAccessRole	inspector:RegisterCrossAccountAccessRole	*
RemoveAttributesFromFindings	inspector:RemoveAttributesFromFindings	*
SetTagsForResource	inspector:SetTagsForResource	*
StartAssessmentRun	inspector:StartAssessmentRun	*
StopAssessmentRun	inspector:StopAssessmentRun	*
SubscribeToEvent	inspector:SubscribeToEvent	*
UnsubscribeFromEvent	inspector:UnsubscribeFromEvent	*
UpdateAssessmentTarget	inspector:UpdateAssessmentTarget	*

Appendix - Amazon Inspector Rules Packages' ARNs

The following is a complete list of ARNs for Amazon Inspector rules packages in all supported regions:

Topics

- US West (Oregon)
- US East (N. Virginia)
- US East (Ohio)
- US West (N. California)
- Asia Pacific (Mumbai)
- Asia Pacific (Sydney)
- Asia Pacific (Seoul)
- Asia Pacific (Tokyo)
- EU (Ireland)
- EU (Frankfurt)
- AWS GovCloud (US)

US West (Oregon)

Rules package name	ARN
Common Vulnerabilities and Exposures	arn:aws:inspector:us-west-2:758058086616:rulespackage/0-9hgA516p
CIS Operating System Security Configuration Benchmarks	arn:aws:inspector:us-west-2:758058086616:rulespackage/0-H5hpSawc
Security Best Practices	arn:aws:inspector:us-west-2:758058086616:rulespackage/0-JJOtZiqQ
Runtime Behavior Analysis	arn:aws:inspector:us-west-2:758058086616:rulespackage/0-vg5GGHSD

US East (N. Virginia)

Rules package name	ARN
Common Vulnerabilities and Exposures	arn:aws:inspector:us-east-1:316112463485:rulespackage/0-gEjTy7T7
CIS Operating System Security Configuration Benchmarks	arn:aws:inspector:us-east-1:316112463485:rulespackage/0-rExsr2X8
Security Best Practices	arn:aws:inspector:us-east-1:316112463485:rulespackage/0-R01qwB5Q
Runtime Behavior Analysis	arn:aws:inspector:us-east-1:316112463485:rulespackage/0-gBONHN9h

US East (Ohio)

Rules package name	ARN
Common Vulnerabilities and Exposures	arn:aws:inspector:us-east-2:646659390643:rulespackage/0-JnA8Zp85

Rules package name	ARN
CIS Operating System Security Configuration Benchmarks	arn:aws:inspector:us-east-2:646659390643:rulespackage/0-m8r61nnh
Security Best Practices	arn:aws:inspector:us-east-2:646659390643:rulespackage/0-AxKmMHPX
Runtime Behavior Analysis	arn:aws:inspector:us-east-2:646659390643:rulespackage/0-UCYZFKPV

US West (N. California)

Rules package name	ARN
Common Vulnerabilities and Exposures	arn:aws:inspector:us-west-1:166987590008:rulespackage/0-TKgzoVOa
CIS Operating System Security Configuration Benchmarks	arn:aws:inspector:us-west-1:166987590008:rulespackage/0-xUY8iRqX
Security Best Practices	arn:aws:inspector:us-west-1:166987590008:rulespackage/0-byoQRFYm
Runtime Behavior Analysis	arn:aws:inspector:us-west-1:166987590008:rulespackage/0-yeYxlt0x

Asia Pacific (Mumbai)

Rules package name	ARN
Common Vulnerabilities and Exposures	arn:aws:inspector:ap-south-1:162588757376:rulespackage/0-LqnJE9dO
CIS Operating System Security Configuration Benchmarks	arn:aws:inspector:ap-south-1:162588757376:rulespackage/0-PSUlX14m
Security Best Practices	arn:aws:inspector:ap-south-1:162588757376:rulespackage/0-fs0IZZBj
Runtime Behavior Analysis	arn:aws:inspector:ap-south-1:162588757376:rulespackage/0-EhMQZy6C

Asia Pacific (Sydney)

Rules package name	ARN
Common Vulnerabilities and Exposures	arn:aws:inspector:ap-southeast-2:454640832652:rulespackage/0-D5TGAxiR
CIS Operating System Security Configuration Benchmarks	arn:aws:inspector:ap-southeast-2:454640832652:rulespackage/0-Vkd2Vxjq
Security Best Practices	arn:aws:inspector:ap-southeast-2:454640832652:rulespackage/0-asL6HRgN
Runtime Behavior Analysis	arn:aws:inspector:ap-southeast-2:454640832652:rulespackage/0-P8Tel2Xj

Asia Pacific (Seoul)

Rules package name	ARN
Common Vulnerabilities and Exposures	arn:aws:inspector:ap-northeast-2:526946625049:rulespackage/0-PoGHMznc
CIS Operating System Security Configuration Benchmarks	arn:aws:inspector:ap-northeast-2:526946625049:rulespackage/0-T9srhg1z
Security Best Practices	arn:aws:inspector:ap-northeast-2:526946625049:rulespackage/0-2WRpmi4n
Runtime Behavior Analysis	arn:aws:inspector:ap-northeast-2:526946625049:rulespackage/0-PoYq7lI7

Asia Pacific (Tokyo)

Rules package name	ARN
Common Vulnerabilities and Exposures	arn:aws:inspector:ap-northeast-1:406045910587:rulespackage/0-gHP9oWNT
CIS Operating System Security Configuration Benchmarks	arn:aws:inspector:ap-northeast-1:406045910587:rulespackage/0-7WNjqgGu
Security Best Practices	arn:aws:inspector:ap-northeast-1:406045910587:rulespackage/0-bBUQnxMq
Runtime Behavior Analysis	arn:aws:inspector:ap-northeast-1:406045910587:rulespackage/0-knGBhqEu

EU (Ireland)

Rules package name	ARN
Common Vulnerabilities and Exposures	arn:aws:inspector:eu-west-1:357557129151:rulespackage/0-ubA5XvBh
CIS Operating System Security Configuration Benchmarks	arn:aws:inspector:eu-west-1:357557129151:rulespackage/0-sJBhCr0F
Security Best Practices	arn:aws:inspector:eu-west-1:357557129151:rulespackage/0-SnojL3Z6
Runtime Behavior Analysis	arn:aws:inspector:eu-west-1:357557129151:rulespackage/0-lLmwe1zd

EU (Frankfurt)

Rules package name	ARN
Common Vulnerabilities and Exposures	arn:aws:inspector:eu-central-1:537503971621:rulespackage/0-wNqHa8M9
CIS Operating System Security Configuration Benchmarks	arn:aws:inspector:eu-central-1:537503971621:rulespackage/0-nZrAVuv8
Security Best Practices	arn:aws:inspector:eu-central-1:537503971621:rulespackage/0-ZujVHEPB

Rules package name	ARN
Runtime Behavior Analysis	arn:aws:inspector:eu-central-1:537503971621:rulespackage/0-0GMUM6fg

AWS GovCloud (US)

Rules package name	ARN
Common Vulnerabilities and Exposures	arn:aws-us-gov:inspector:us-gov-west-1:850862329162:rulespackage/0-4oQgcI4G
CIS Operating System Security Configuration Benchmarks	arn:aws-us-gov:inspector:us-gov-west-1:850862329162:rulespackage/0-Ac4CFOuc
Security Best Practices	arn:aws-us-gov:inspector:us-gov-west-1:850862329162:rulespackage/0-rOTGqe5G
Runtime Behavior Analysis	arn:aws-us-gov:inspector:us-gov-west-1:850862329162:rulespackage/0-JMyjuzoW

Document History

Latest documentation update: June 13, 2018

The following table describes the documentation release history of Amazon Inspector after May 2018.

Change	Description	Date
Added region support	Added region support for AWS GovCloud (US)	June 13, 2018

The following table describes the documentation release history of Amazon Inspector before June 2018.

Change	Description	Date
New content	Added the ability to target all Amazon EC2 instances in an account. For more information, see Amazon Inspector Assessment Targets.	May 24, 2018
Added OS support	Added Amazon Inspector support for Amazon Linux 2018.03 and Ubuntu 18.04	May 15, 2018
New content	Added ability to set up recurring Amazon Inspector assessments.	April 30, 2018
New content	Added ability to install an Amazon Inspector agent through the Inspector console.	April 30, 2018
Added OS support	Added Amazon Inspector support for Amazon Linux 2.	March 13, 2018
Added OS support	Added Amazon Inspector assessment support for Windows 2016.	February 20, 2018

Change	Description	Date
Added region support	Added Amazon Inspector support for the Ohio (CMH) region.	February 7, 2018
New content	Amazon Inspector assessments can now run when the kernal module is unavailable.	January 11, 2018
Added region support	Added Amazon Inspector support for the Frankfurt (FRA) region.	December 19, 2017
New content	Added ability to check Amazon Inspector agent health with the Amazon Inspector API and console.	December 15, 2017
New content	Added the following features: [See the AWS documentation website for more details]	December 5, 2017
Added OS support	Added Amazon Inspector assessment support for CentOS 7.4.	November 9, 2017
Added OS support	Added Amazon Inspector assessment support for Amazon Linux 2017.09.	October 11, 2017
Added OS support	Added Amazon Inspector assessment support for RHEL 7.4.	February 20, 2018
Added HIPAA eligability	Amazon Inspector is now HIPAA eligable.	July 31, 2017
New content	Added ability to automatically trigger Amazon Inspector security assessment with Amazon CloudWatch Events	July 27, 2017
Added region support	Added Amazon Inspector support for the San Francisco (SFO) region.	June 6, 2018
Added OS support	Added Amazon Inspector assessment support for RHEL 6.2-6.9, RHEL 7.2-7.3, CentOS 6.9, and CentOS 7.2-7.3.	May 23, 2017
Added OS support	Added Amazon Inspector assessment support for Amazon Linux 2017.03.	April 25, 2017
New content and added OS support	Added: [See the AWS documentation website for more details]	January 5, 2017
New OS support	Added Amazon Inspector support for Microsoft Windows.	August 26, 2016
Added region support	Added Amazon Inspector support for the Asia Pacific (Seoul) region.	August 26, 2016
Added region support	Added Amazon Inspector support for the Asia Pacific (Mumbai) region.	April 25, 2016

Change	Description	Date
Added region support	Added Amazon Inspector support for the Asia Pacific (Sydney)	April 25, 2016
Service launch	Amazon Inspector serviced launched.	Oct 7, 2015

www.ingramcontent.com/pod-product-compliance
Lightning Source LLC
LaVergne TN
LVHW082041050326
832904LV00005B/260